BALTIMORE'S CAST-IRON BUILDINGS
AND ARCHITECTURAL IRONWORK

300 West Pratt Street.

BALTIMORE'S CAST-IRON BUILDINGS AND ARCHITECTURAL IRONWORK

James D. Dilts and Catharine F. Black, Editors

With photographs by Ron Haisfield

Published in association with Baltimore Heritage, Inc., by

TIDEWATER PUBLISHERS
Centreville, Maryland

Library of Congress Cataloging-in-Publication Data

Baltimore's cast-iron buildings and architectural ironwork / James D.
  Dilts and Catharine F. Black, editors. –1st ed.
      p. cm.
   "Published in association with Baltimore Heritage, Inc."
   Includes bibliographical references and index.
   ISBN 0-87033-427-1 (pbk.) :
   1. Cast-iron fronts (Architecture)—Maryland—Baltimore.
  2. Architectural ironwork—Maryland—Baltimore   3. Baltimore (Md.)—
  Buildings, structures, etc.   I. Dilts, James D.
  II. Black, Catharine F. (Catharine Foster)
  NA735.B3B35   1991
  721'.0447141'09752609034—dc20   91-50583
                                                          CIP

Photos: Cover—300 West Pratt Street
          p. i—The Abell Building, 329-335 West Baltimore Street
          p. v—Detail, 307-309 West Baltimore Street
          p. xiv—Detail, 307-309 West Baltimore Street
          p. 1—322 West Baltimore Street

Map on pages 100-101 used with permission of ADC The Map People®. Except in chapter V (see page 47), all photographs, unless otherwise noted, are by Ron Haisfield © 1991.

Manufactured in the United States of America
First edition, 1991; second printing, 2000

CONTENTS

The segmental cast-iron dome of George A. Frederick's Baltimore City Hall rises high over the nearby rooftops in this view looking north along Holliday Street. Wendel Bollman, the engineer and bridge builder who helped Frederick design the dome, and the Bartlett, Robbins & Co. foundry both supplied the ironwork. Circa late 1870s photo: Jack and Beverly Wilgus Collection.

Foreword

BALTIMORE AND ITS CAST-IRON ARCHITECTURE

by
Margot Gayle

It is hard to believe, but in the whole United States, only four historic buildings with total facades of cast iron have been fully restored. Baltimore can assert with pride that it possesses one of these four. It is, of course, the 1871 Wilkens-Robins Building at 300 West Pratt Street.

Now renamed the Marsh & McLennan Building, the restored, five-story iron-front former warehouse has taken on a certain majesty. With a gleaming new coat of white paint, its wide expanses of glass windows freshly glazed, and the whole set off by modern wings built on either side, the successful ensemble is an asset to the Inner Harbor area.

As can be seen at a glance, this regenerated building exemplifies a happy marriage of nineteenth- and twentieth-century construction methods. Furthermore, it provides a case history of what can result from the cooperation of adventurous developers, innovative architects, persistent preservationists, and such groups as Baltimore Heritage and Friends of Cast Iron Architecture, especially when they can make common cause with sophisticated public officials such as then-mayor William Donald Schaefer, who held off demolition demands until a feasible restoration and financing proposal could be brought forward.

For the record, the other three totally restored iron fronts in the United States are the ornate Grand Opera House in Wilmington, Delaware; the old Sterns Block in Richmond, Virginia, that row of four handsome iron facades looking-like-one on East Main Street, united now to form a modern, air-conditioned office building known simply as "The Ironfronts"; and the Smythe Stores condominium apartments on lower Arch Street

in Philadelphia, where an innovative conversion has turned a row of five 1857 identical iron-front commercial buildings into a tree-planted block in "Old City."

Oddly enough there are ties to Baltimore in two of these cast-iron buildings in nearby Eastern Seaboard cities. The Opera House was designed as the Wilmington Masonic Temple in 1871 by a well-known firm of Baltimore architects, Charles L. Carson and Thomas Dixon. "The Ironfronts" were erected in Richmond in 1866 to designs of an English architect named George H. Johnson, then residing in Baltimore, who had the iron components for this good-looking row of fronts cast in Baltimore's famous Hayward, Bartlett foundry. An additional tie between these two restorations and the Marsh & McLennan effort is that all were accomplished through the skills of Steven T. Baird's company of architects and metal specialists located in Salt Lake City.

Looking back, we can see that Baltimore has always had a worthwhile share of the nation's heritage of cast-iron architecture. It began with that great pioneer example, the Baltimore Sun's Iron Building, now gone, whose history is recounted in depth here by David Wright. Baltimore's prize example in the present is that premier instance of interior structural and ornamental cast iron which anyone can visit by merely stepping through an entrance on Mount Vernon Place. I refer, of course, to the many-galleried Peabody Library, which is explored in this book through the

---

Margot Gayle, president of the Friends of Cast Iron Architecture, is co-author, with Edmund V. Gillon, Jr., of Cast-Iron Architecture in New York.

scholarly research of Phoebe Stanton. Not far away is the high-reaching dome of City Hall, which Baltimoreans saved and restored by supporting the city's 1974 bond issue for renovation. Additionally, there are the many instances of decorative ironwork on Baltimore streets that provide visual pleasure to all, especially to Robert Alexander, who records them in words and photographs.

From 1850 onward, Baltimore had a remarkable number of other iron-front buildings positioned along the streets of its commercial neighborhoods. This nineteenth-century heritage was first diminished when many iron-front buildings were destroyed in the Great Fire of 1904, among them the historic 1851 Sun Building and its neighbor, the 1876 mansard-roofed Baltimore American Building. Then, half a century later, perhaps a dozen significant iron-front structures were taken down—with few if any voices raised to save them—in the urban renewal drive that cleared land for Charles Center. Others were eliminated in the 1970s for the Inner Harbor redevelopment that included the Convention Center. The latter now occupies the site of the former Fava Fruit Company's iron building, doggedly championed by David Wright and disassembled by the city for future re-erection as part of the Baltimore City Life Museums.

The really good news is that some ten iron fronts still stand on Baltimore streets, and that most seem to be structurally sound, worthy candidates for restorative treatment. Among them are some very interesting examples of nineteenth-century iron architecture that would be the envy of certain American cities that have seen their iron buildings rather carelessly destroyed—for instance, St. Louis, where in the course of creating Gateway National Park with its soaring stainless steel arch, ever so many well-designed iron commercial buildings on forty acres beside the levee were taken down. A few were dismantled and stored, but later on even those were mindlessly smashed with a bulldozer.

Baltimoreans should not be discouraged because existing iron fronts on West Baltimore Street (and the one at 121 North Howard Street, for instance) seem drab and display harshly altered ground floors. There are ways to handle that. First, look at this book's Directory of Baltimore's cast-iron buildings (I am particularly attracted to 322 and 414 West Baltimore Street). Then take heart by recalling how forlorn the Wilkens-Robins Building looked for nearly a decade, its windows boarded up, decorative iron acanthus

Detail from the Sterns Block. Photo: Katherine Wetzel.

The Sterns Block, now known as "The Ironfronts," at 1007-1013 East Main Street, Richmond, built circa 1865, was cast by Baltimore's Hayward, Bartlett & Co. The Tredegar Iron Works in Richmond, armorer to the Confederacy, along with 900 other buildings in the city, was destroyed in the evacuation fire during the final days of the Civil War. A cast-iron facade, prefabricated and shipped from out of town, offered a quick way to rebuild. Photo: Katherine Wetzel.

The Branch Building, next door at 1015 East Main Street, built circa 1866, was also cast by Hayward, Bartlett & Co. to designs by the architect of the Sterns Block, George H. Johnson, who formerly worked for Daniel Badger's famous architectural ironworks in New York. The building has a ground-floor arcade, and now houses a brokerage. Photo: Katherine Wetzel.

leaves stripped from its column capitals, and raw brick walls exposed on either side where neighboring buildings once stood.

As engineer and foundry manager Scott Howell tells us, every iron front is the sum of its precast iron elements produced in a foundry, where they were machined smooth, primed for protection from moisture, then fastened together to form panels and modules. Delivered to a construction site, these were lifted and bolted into position, constituting the front of the waiting, conventionally constructed, multistoried building with side and rear walls of common brick.

Such a facade could be of very plain design, or could be replete with such decorative features as columns, ornamented window caps, keystones, and projecting cornices held on brackets. The result was often quite stunning.

No one ever told it better than Robert P. Winthrop in his book, *Cast & Wrought: The Architectural Ironwork of Richmond, Virginia*: "The elaboration, complexity and sheer weight of decoration of these iron facades is remarkable [yet] . . . they are significant works of architecture, not merely decorated walls . . . The technical achievement represented by the Sterns Block is extraordinary. To make [its] 60 columns and their elaborate capitals required assembling 1,920 pieces. The facade contains over 5,000 visible pieces."

Whether it be plain or ornate, one of the best aspects of cast-iron architecture is the way it lends itself to restoration. No need to match old brick or seek stones from a long-closed quarry; no need to recarve eroded designs. Simply cast new pieces out of metal. Where structural needs demand it, these should be cast iron. However, in some instances, replacement parts can be cast aluminum, a remarkable metal that was not even available when the nineteenth-century iron-front buildings were erected. For casting purposes aluminum melts at a lower temperature than ferrous alloys, and thus demands less energy and causes less pollution. Furthermore, it is not subject to rust. However, as Howell points out, iron and aluminum parts must be kept insulated from one another, as is the case with all metals, to avoid electrolytic interaction.

One carefully prepared pattern often suffices for recasting many missing pieces, perhaps a row of identical columns, or several missing quoins or acanthus leaves. Once these are bolted into place with today's stainless steel fasteners (following a careful job of cleaning and caulking), and once a reliable primer has been applied along with a coat of compatible modern paint, well, a building can look like new. And it can keep that new look for a long, long time.

James Bogardus knew this and stressed it in his influential pamphlet, entitled *Cast Iron Buildings: Their Construction and Advantages*, that helped win appreciation in this country for iron architecture. He was the inventive New York architect-engineer who had devoted himself in the 1840s to advocating cast-iron construction in the United States. This was after his 1836 trip to England where a few decades earlier Britishers had worked out the breakthrough technology for producing structural cast iron in quantity at a cost that made it a practical building material. Bogardus finally got his chance to demonstrate its value to Americans in 1848 when he was commissioned to build the row of iron Laing Stores in downtown Manhattan.

Detail, Donnan Block. Photo: Katherine Wetzel.

The success of this example attracted, as it happened, perhaps through press accounts, the interest of Baltimore publisher A. S. Abell, who turned to Bogardus in 1849 for the erection of a state-of-the-art publishing center for his Baltimore *Sun* newspaper, whose amazing iron structure was completed in 1851. These two structures in two different cities, the first with iron walls, the second with both iron frame and iron walls, marked early steady steps toward development of the skyscraper.

Bogardus went on to construct elsewhere a number of tall iron structures, including an iron lighthouse, two iron fire lookout towers, and two iron shot towers. (Baltimore, with its landmark brick shot tower, may be the only city in our country where that term needs no explanation. For non-natives, however, a brief description: From the top of a shot tower molten lead was poured through a sieve. As the drops fell, they

Noting its proximity, date, and style, Richmond historians believe that the city's Donnan Block, at 1207-1211 East Main Street, built circa 1866, was also designed by George H. Johnson and founded by Hayward, Bartlett & Co. Photo: Katherine Wetzel.

The answer is less elusive when one understands that in former ages iron was available in amounts sufficient for making a multitude of small items, but was definitely not available until modern times in large quantities at a cost that allowed it even to be considered for construction projects such as bridges, piers, viaducts, factories, and storehouses. Medieval cathedrals got built somehow without metal, and so did castles in Spain and, before that, aqueducts in Rome.

It was in 1779 that the Darby family's foundry completed the world's first bridge made of iron, spanning the Severn River in the north of England. Pedestrians could cross it, as could hay wagons, cattle, and horses. This landmark bridge still exists and, after its restoration, England's Prince Charles rededicated it on its 200th anniversary.

Soon after the Severn River's Ironbridge was in place, cast iron was introduced in 1792 for fire-resistant pillars to replace wooden ones in fire-plagued English cotton mills, then for pillars supporting galleries in churches and theaters, both in England and in the United States; soon it was used as supports for ground-floor iron shopfronts in France and England and especially in America where the iron storefront became an all-time favorite.

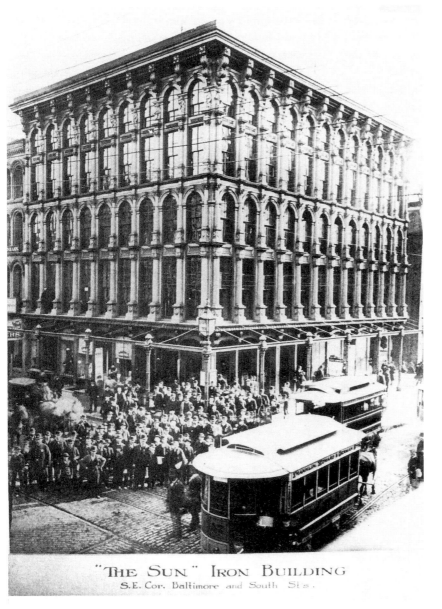

"THE SUN" IRON BUILDING

S.E. Cor. Baltimore and South Sts.

The staff holds up traffic in the street to pose in front of the Sun Iron Building, by James Bogardus. Circa 1880 photo: The Baltimore Sun.

The use of metal for larger purposes than nails, tie rods, hinges, and bolts was spreading, but it took a while. It also took such inventive minds as that of Bogardus, and others to follow, to envision the possibility of making entire exterior walls of cast iron, and also to envision interior skeletal frames of metal to support them, or to achieve great heights as in the case of lighthouses.

became round shot and solidified upon hitting a pool of cold water at ground level.) In Baltimore, he also constructed, in 1852 and 1853, two five-story iron-front commercial buildings, now gone, which were among the earliest anywhere. Undoubtedly the link between James Bogardus and Baltimore is strong.

The question sometimes arises as to why, early in the nineteenth century, cast iron seemed suddenly to become a much-used metal, yet after only a few decades seemed almost as suddenly to be no longer in demand.

Multistoried walls of iron needed only to be demonstrated, and threats of lightning strikes and collapse debunked, for them to be appreciated by the American construction industry. Their resistance to fire attracted builders in cities that had experienced large urban fires. Their light weight, compared to thick stone walls, reduced foundation requirements as well as allowed more interior floor space, making the very thin iron street walls even more attractive. So did their speed of construction, and the fact that iron walls could be ornamented in the course of the casting process.

Cast iron was used most intensively for about fifty years, from the 1840s until nearly the end of the nineteenth century, and to a lesser degree until about the time of the Great Depression. (In my investigations in New York, I have documented a final iron front erected in 1904.) In midtown Manhattan I can point out one Beaux Arts style office building after another, still standing near Grand Central Station, where architects relied on cast iron for window enframements of large glass areas in masonry walls, for canopies, and for decorative lobby metalwork. A Baltimore example is the 1894 Equitable Building at Calvert and Fayette streets, with its beautiful cast-iron window surrounds and apron panels.

At any rate, by the turn of the twentieth century, a more versatile metal, introduced for large construction in 1885, had become fully available at a cost-effective price. That metal was steel.

And that, in a nutshell, is why, over a very short time span, cast iron with its welcome structural advantages became widely used, making the Industrial Revolution possible, then was superseded by steel.

I once coined a sentence in a lecture which went like this: "Cast iron was the gift of the eighteenth century to the nineteenth century, and steel was the gift of the nineteenth century to the twentieth." It seems to sum it up.

The 105-foot-long cast-iron facade of the Fava Fruit Company Building, 218-226 South Charles Street, built circa 1869, was the largest remaining in the city when it was taken down in 1976. Restored by Steven T. Baird, Architect and Associates of Salt Lake City, the iron front awaits re-erection as part of the Baltimore City Life Museums. 1970 photo: The Peale Museum, Baltimore City Life Museums.

Now cast iron is primarily employed for restorative purposes, for security grilles and gates, for such street furniture as period lampposts, and for decorative fences, fountains, and the like in the landscape.

To close on a note of caution, those disassembled iron parts of the historic Fava Fruit Company's building, so painstakingly dismantled, should be guarded with care wherever they are stored, presumably cleaned, primed, and numbered for re-erection. Few, if any, iron fronts that have been dismantled have ever been resurrected, so here again Baltimore may establish a first. The loss of the iron parts of the first iron-front building anywhere, the 1849 Laing Stores in Manhattan, is still clear in my mind. It was 1974 when they were discovered by thieves who broke them up for ready handling and carted them off for scrap.

Although the upper floors at 17 South Howard Street were burned out, business as usual goes on in the storefront; the buildings on either side, also iron fronts, appear not to have been damaged, a good illustration of cast iron's fire resistance. 1931 photo: The Peale Museum, Baltimore City Life Museums.

Preface

by
James D. Dilts
and Catharine F. Black

In the years since *Baltimore's Cast-Iron Buildings and Architectural Ironwork* was published in 1991, what served initially as a brief exposition, directory, and guidebook has become a historical resource. For that reason we and Tidewater Publishers have decided to reprint the book, which has been out of print for some time, with only minor editorial corrections and changes.

During the previous decade, the city lost two of its ten full cast-iron front buildings, the ones at 412 and 414 West Baltimore Street. Both were significant losses: the first (412) was a pre–Civil War building, the oldest ironfront then standing; its neighbor at 414 was closely associated with Baltimore's most famous writer, H. L. Mencken. The two structures were demolished in 1998 following a series of unfortunate events, some of them avoidable.

We also lost two iron storefront buildings. This year 423 West Baltimore Street, with a cast-iron storefront and a unique sheet-metal facade, was badly damaged by fire and demolished. Another building, the former firehouse at 1031 West Mulberry Street with a cast-iron ground floor, was demolished this year but not before its ironwork was salvaged, although the present whereabouts of the iron elements are unknown.

But there have been some positive developments as well since the book first appeared. We gained one full cast-iron facade when the former Fava Fruit Company Building (mentioned at the conclusion of Margot Gayle's Foreword, page xii) was reerected in 1996. Designed in a new configuration by architects Peterson and Brickbauer, the building functioned briefly as an exhibit center of the Baltimore City Life Museums.

Unfortunately, the museums closed due to lack of funds in 1997. The building's new private owners anticipate turning it into a conference center, art gallery, and restaurant. (Since Margot Gayle's essay was written, several more existing buildings with complete cast-iron facades, many of them in New York's Soho district, have been fully restored, following the examples of Baltimore's 300 West Pratt Street and similar restorations in a handful of other cities.)

The Rombro Building (page 72) has in the interim been converted into an office building for federal agencies and its ground-floor cast-iron storefront sensitively restored. The Abell Building (page 73), owned by the same owners, is to be made into apartments; we hope that the plans include the restoration of its unique ground-floor ironwork, the most extensive such installation in the city. And the former commercial building at 118-120 North Paca Street (page 79), which stood empty in 1991, has been renovated as part of Paca House, a single-room-occupancy complex for the homeless.

The significance of the remaining structures to Baltimore, an American center of cast-iron architecture, has only increased. A century ago in the city, there were more than a hundred iron-front buildings, according to an informed estimate by author David G. Wright, who has researched a great many of the original structures. The Baltimore fire of 1904 destroyed dozens of them. In 1962, based on an actual count by author Phoebe B. Stanton, there were still thirty-six buildings with full iron facades standing on Baltimore's streets. Since then the majority of them have fallen to downtown redevelopment projects. Including the recent gains and losses, there are now only nine left.

These survivors, along with the fifteen additional iron storefronts documented here, are still clearly an endangered species, especially considering the events of the past decade. Most of these ironfronts are now on the National Register of Historic Places, appropriately enough, because they represent an architecture of unique clarity and articulation, structural innovation, and historical importance.

Several individuals contributed their valuable time and energy to make the Baltimore cast-iron architecture project a reality. In the beginning, Baltimore Heritage board members Steve Israel, Mike Isekoff, the late Walter Fisher, and Helen Davis helped with research, and the late Bix Leonard and the late Henry Naylor with photography. The late Libbie Hartley did research as well. Fred B. Shoken, then president of Baltimore Heritage, and Janet Davis, Carolyn Donkervoet, Lun Harris, Lisa Jensen, Dean Krimmel, Karen Lewand, John Maclay, the late Morgan Pritchett, Romaine Somerville, and Sandy Sparks, all present or former board members, assisted us with planning, documentation, fund-raising, and design. Sadly we note the death of one of our authors, Robert L. Alexander, whose knowledge of and enthusiasm for Baltimore's historic architecture and ironwork originally inspired the writing of this book.

The early support of Judy D. Dobbs and Barbara W. Sarudy of the Maryland Humanities Council was crucial to our success. Charles T. Lyle, former president of the Maryland Historical Society, and George H. Callcott, former chairman of its publications committee, aided our efforts. Margot Gayle, Robert Vogel, David Wright, and Carlos P. Avery gave us useful guidance and advice; Penny Williamson provided constant support; and Aaron Levin supplied valuable documentary photographs. We are grateful to the George Peabody Library of the Johns Hopkins University for permission to reprint the Hayward, Bartlett and the Bartlett, Robbins catalogs. We thank our current sponsors, The Baltimore Architecture Foundation and the Maryland Historical Trust, for their financial support of this reprint. Finally, to Peter E. Kurtze, who did the concluding research, and especially to photographer Ron Haisfield, whose images accounted in large part for the success of the initial publication, we owe our special thanks for a job well done.

Original publication of this book was made possible by grants from

Maryland Humanities Council
William G. Baker, Jr., Memorial Fund
The Baltimore Foundation for Architecture, Inc.
The Lois and Irving Blum Foundation, Inc.
Morton and Sophia Macht Foundation, Inc.
Marsh & McLennan, Inc.
Maryland Historical Society
The Maryland National Foundation, Inc.
The Rouse Company Foundation
Signet Bank
Stone & Associates, Inc.
Stiles E. Tuttle Trust
Union Trust Bank

The 2000 reprint was made possible by additional support from

The Baltimore Architecture Foundation
Maryland Historical Trust

BALTIMORE'S CAST-IRON BUILDINGS
AND ARCHITECTURAL IRONWORK

A metal fence guards the city's venerable Battle Monument, and a lacy three-story cast-iron portico on the St. Clair Hotel watches over the square in this Baltimore photo from the 1860s-1870s. The portico was cast by Baltimore's most important architectural foundry: Hayward, Bartlett & Co. Photo: Ross J. Kelbaugh Collection.

Part One

I. INTRODUCTION

by
James D. Dilts

The fourth most common element on the earth's surface also forms the core of the planet and even falls from the skies. Primitive man refined meteorites, which consist of almost pure iron, into tools and weapons. Ubiquitous and cheap, not a "precious metal," it is still an element of the greatest value and utility in our modern urban society. Iron provides the essentials of our transportation systems (automobile engine blocks and subway rails), the structural core of our downtown office buildings, and the basis of our armaments, the atavistic tools of death and destruction.

Iron occurs naturally in our food and water; indeed, it is an important component of our blood. No other material substance is more intimately involved with daily existence or has more profoundly influenced human destiny. Iron long ago entered the realm of metaphor: a forceful person is a "ball of fire"; we must "strike while the iron is hot"; an individual has an "iron will," "nerves of steel," or a "cast-iron stomach."

Human beings first made iron into beads and daggers more than 5,000 years ago. The Egyptians and Assyrians, the Greeks and Romans, and later Asians and Western Europeans used small amounts of both cast and wrought iron. Expressive as well as strong, it has long been associated with art. The Chinese cast iron into statues in the eighth century, and in the seventeenth, created wrought-iron pictures that they mounted in frames or windows. The beautiful wrought-iron cathedral screens of Renaissance Spain—rejas—and Italy and France, are well known. The Germans in the early 1800s wore cast-iron jewelry. Americans of

the 1850s studied photographic images on iron sheets known as tintypes.

But iron's major function has always been utilitarian. The oldest piece of cast iron in England is a grave slab dating to 1350. Other uses followed—protective devices such as fences, gates, and locks, as well as common household items: stoves, firebacks, and utensils—until the Industrial Revolution. After that, the material burst forth in the hands of Victorian-era engineers and architects to become everything from bridges to entire buildings. In architecture, its structural and decorative qualities were utilized to full advantage.

There are important differences between cast iron (formed in a mold) and wrought iron (worked by hand or machine), beginning with the processes of production. The early furnace used for smelting ore, known as a Catalan forge, was a crude rock structure with a primitive bellows, sometimes operated by water power. Charged with charcoal, iron ore, and limestone, then fired for several hours, it yielded a white-hot metallic mass, literally a ball of fire. After it was removed from the forge and pounded with a 500-pound tilt-hammer (possibly also water-powered) to expel the slag amidst a shower of sparks, the result was basic wrought iron, a ferrous alloy containing virtually no carbon.

This was further refined, through repeated heating and hammering, into a "bloom" of iron. Forges that did this were often called "bloomeries." By the 1700s, the blooms were being rolled mechanically into "merchant bars" for sale to blacksmiths who reheated and pounded them on their anvils into horseshoes and dozens of domestic products. Or the bars were flattened into sheets for use as boiler plate, or passed through a slitting mill to be cut into nails.

With the addition of a high stack to the rudimentary Catalan forge and improvement of the bellows, blast furnaces were developed in the Middle Ages. As the furnaces grew bigger and hotter, some of the iron ore dissolved carbon from the charcoal, and fused with it to form a liquid, which accidentally ran out the bottom of the furnace. Sometime later, it was discovered that the molten metal, or cast iron, could be channeled into a trough, and made to enter sand molds so arranged that they looked like a nursing litter of pigs, hence the name pig iron. Cast iron was also a ferrous alloy, high in carbon content. Each pig weighed roughly 100 pounds, for that was about all a man could lift. The pigs were destined for a foundry to be remelted and cast into final form: a kitchen pot or a cannon. Gradually pig iron replaced the glowing ball of wrought iron as the major product of the early furnaces, and it became a staple of commerce.

Cast and wrought iron vary greatly in their composition and characteristics, and therefore in the ways in which they are used. Cast iron contains from 2 to 6 percent carbon; wrought iron, a tiny fraction of 1 percent. Modern steel, another ferrous alloy, contains about .5 percent carbon.

High carbon content gives cast iron its great compressive strength, for it is capable of withstanding a downward force of some forty tons per square inch. In tension, however, it is relatively weak, able to support about fifteen tons per square inch.

Wrought iron is just the opposite, possessing roughly half the compressive strength of cast iron, but about double its tensile strength. For the sake of comparison, steel is four times as strong as cast iron in compression, and has twice the power of wrought iron in tension.

The carbon distributed through cast iron makes it brittle, and not malleable, although it can be machined. But cast iron is highly plastic, and will assume any form in a mold. However, if dropped from a height or struck with a hammer, it will break. In that regard it most resembles stone, and a fracture reveals a granular composition, like granite. Therefore, the most appropriate architectural use for cast iron was as a column or decorative element.

Wrought iron, containing an infinitesimal amount of carbon, is actually hardened by hammering in the forge. It is highly ductile and in addition to forging can be rolled into rails or drawn into wire. Wrought iron is fibrous in nature and has a grain, like wood. It was therefore sometimes employed as beams in nine-

"Bartlett, Robbins & Co. Late Hayward, Bartlett & Co., Architectural Iron Works, Designers and Manufacturers of complete equipment for municipal gas works. Iron fronts, verandas, balconies, complete summer houses, light houses. A large number of first-class iron buildings have been erected by us in Baltimore as well as in New York, Richmond, Raleigh, New Orleans, Galveston and as far as Portland, Oregon," read the firm's exhibit sign at the Philadelphia Exposition of 1876. From the foundry at Pratt and Scott streets, iron fronts were also shipped to Havana, the Midwest, and around Cape Horn to Seattle. Illus.: George W. Howard, The Monumental City, *Baltimore, 1873.*

The G. R. Vickers Office Building, an iron front by Bartlett, Robbins & Co., stood on German (Redwood) Street near South Street, site of the present Vickers Building. Illus.: Howard's Monumental City.

teenth-century buildings, but its relatively high cost prohibited widespread use.

There was an ancient method of producing crucible steel by heating wrought-iron bars with charcoal in a closed furnace for days—so that the metal absorbed some of the carbon—and then fusing the bars in a clay and graphite crucible, but such steel was so costly that it was used only for weapons and special tools requiring superior strength and hardness.

Metallurgy, a complex science, is mainly devoted either to changing the chemical composition of the material or altering its form by mechanical means. Often these processes take place in tandem, and slight deviations in the rate of heating and cooling (annealing), for example, can profoundly affect the result. For much of the nineteenth century, ironmaking was more an art than a science.

As pig iron became the basic product of the blast furnace, technological developments were directed towards getting rid of its carbon and other impurities by oxidizing them to create wrought iron. One way to do this was in a puddling furnace, a horizontal, reverberatory furnace developed in England in the 1780s, whose heat radiated down from the roof, as in a kiln (in contrast to rising vertically, as in a blast furnace).

When pig iron was combined with iron ore and cinder in the hearth, which was itself lined with iron, and then heated to about 2,500 degrees Fahrenheit, the impurities formed slag. In the final stages, puddlers (laborers) stationed at the working doors, armed with long hooks, rabbled (raked) frantically at the boiling mass, working the material into a glowing ball of iron weighing 100 to 200 pounds, like that which emerged from the medieval Catalan forge. It would then be squeezed flat, cut, reheated, and rolled into marketable form. The daily output of such a furnace was about a ton of iron. The puddlers were the aristocrats of the iron industry. By necessity, they possessed great skill, strength, and endurance, and commanded high wages.

Similarly, pig iron was converted into refined iron for casting in a foundry cupola furnace, invented in the 1790s. This was a blast furnace filled with a column of coke, pig iron, and limestone. The last served as a flux, or detergent, to scour out and fuse the impurities so they would run off as slag. The cupola furnace was fired by a blast of air forced in through holes called tuyeres at the bottom. As the iron melted, it was drawn out and poured into molds.

In the mid-nineteenth century, these practices began to change. By forcing air through a great number of tuyere holes in the bottom of a clay-lined retort, the Bessemer converter, developed about 1856, could transform twenty tons of pig iron into steel in ten minutes with a roaring, brilliant pyrotechnic display. The Siemens open-hearth process, where steel was made in an improved reverberatory furnace, was invented around a decade later. To accompany these new methods, there was a major new source of American iron: Lake Superior's Mesabi range shipped its first ore in 1854.

Still, it took sixty to seventy-five years for the new technology to be adopted and the old to die out completely. Locally, in 1887, the Maryland Steel Company at Sparrows Point began the erection of four blast furnaces to convert iron ore into pig iron, and later added facilities to make Bessemer and open-hearth steel. However, the state's production of high-grade charcoal iron in what were basically Catalan forges lingered on until 1915 when the last forge closed. In the meantime, the railroad had become a key factor in the progress of iron.

Iron, coal, and the steam engine were the major ingredients of the Industrial Revolution, and in the early nineteenth century, first in England, then in America, they coalesced in the railroad. The ways in which the Darbys, the great British ironmasters, the Wilkinsons, fabricators of precision steam cylinders, and the Stephensons, renowned coalfield engineers, reinforced each other's work to create the railroad are both intricate and fascinating. The railroad awakened the iron industry by stimulating demand, and by providing the means to assemble the raw materials and distribute the products.

The British Industrial Revolution ran a century to a generation ahead of the American one until the 1850s. Abraham Darby began smelting iron ore with coke, rather than charcoal, in 1735; the first successful iron-producing coke furnace in the United States was operated at Lonaconing, Maryland, in 1839. The Darbys made the castings for the famous iron bridge at Coalbrookdale, the first such structure in the world, in 1779. The first American iron bridge was constructed on the National Road, in Brownsville, Pennsylvania, also in 1839. John Birkinshaw rolled the first British wrought-iron rail (basically a T-rail), in 1820. The first American wrought-iron T-rail was rolled at Maryland's Mount Savage ironworks near Cumberland in 1845.

England preceded the United States in the architectural use of iron as well. The world's first multistory iron-framed building was William Strutt's calico mill constructed in 1792 in Derby, England, with cast-iron

Another Bartlett, Robbins iron front, built for tobacco merchant L. W. Gunther, was at 9 South Gay Street. Illus.: Howard's Monumental City.

columns and beams. British bridge builders were employing wrought-iron beams in the 1830s and there were isolated instances of their use in construction. English engineer William Fairbairn, in 1839, prefabricated an all-iron building three stories high, with a framework of cast and wrought iron and a corrugated iron roof; James Bogardus saw it assembled in London before it was shipped to Constantinople for use as a flour mill.

But by midcentury, America was catching up. In 1854, while Fairbairn advocated in print the general use of wrought-iron beams in buildings, the first such beams manufactured in America were being installed in New York's Harper and Brothers publishing house, Cooper Union, and other structures. They had been rolled the previous year in Peter Cooper's Trenton ironworks, and were identical to a railroad T-rail.

Actually, on either side of the Atlantic in the same year—1851—two new buildings appeared, one in London and the other in Baltimore that, though vastly different in scale, were equally indicative of things to come. They were not the first of their kind, but rather prototypes. Both were destroyed by fire in this century.

Joseph Paxton's Crystal Palace, built for the Great London Exposition, was an iron-framed, glass-covered pavilion, basically a plant conservatory, but on a huge scale. Charles Dickens recounted its awesome statistics: 1,851 feet long (the same number as the year) and 450 feet wide, covering 18 acres. Its iron skeleton consisted of 3,300 hollow columns, 2,224 girders, and 1,128 supporting units for the galleries. The glass alone weighed 400 tons. The three-story prefabricated structure, crowned by a barrel vault, was erected in seventeen weeks, and created a sensation. (Taken down, moved, and rebuilt at Sydenham, the Crystal Palace was damaged by fire in 1936, and finally demolished in 1941.)

J. W. Bond and Company conducted a book business from their stylish iron front at 90 Baltimore Street, which was manufactured by Bartlett, Robbins & Co. Illus.: Howard's Monumental City.

In Baltimore, A. S. Abell intended his new Sun Iron Building to be "the finest newspaper office in America." When the five-story structure opened at the corner of Baltimore and South streets in the fall of 1851, it had two full iron facades and an internal support system of cast-iron columns and beams. The Sun Iron Building was the initial, large-scale commercial application of James Bogardus's system of all-iron construction. (Bogardus, as a practical matter, invented the cast-iron front.) Besides Bogardus, architect Robert G. Hatfield and iron founder Daniel D. Badger were also involved with the project, which received international attention. (The Sun Iron Building, one of the monuments of American cast-iron architecture, perished in the Great Baltimore Fire of 1904.)

By the time the Sun Building was completed, the local iron industry was well prepared for the deluge of orders for similar buildings that followed. Serendipitously, Baltimore's season for cast-iron architecture that began in the 1850s coincided with the beginning of the peak period of Maryland's iron production. The Baltimore and Ohio Railroad had connected the city and its numerous furnaces, forges, and foundries, some of them dating from colonial days, with the newly developed coalfields and ironworks of Western Maryland. In 1855, there were twenty-six furnaces throughout the state making 30,000 tons of pig iron annually, a tenfold increase over the preceding twenty-five years.

The increase was due mainly to the railroad. Baltimore's ironworks since the 1830s had supplied cast-iron steam cylinders, journal boxes, and wheels, along with wrought-iron frames, boilers, axles, rods, valve gears, and other major items for its locomotives and cars. In the following decade, they made rails for the B&O. The railroad was installing cast-iron columns in trestles at Harpers Ferry by that time, and the material was beginning to be used structurally in Baltimore churches.

In 1851, at the same time that Bogardus, Hatfield, and Badger, the big names in cast-iron architecture, were working on the Sun Iron Building, a dozen blocks to the west at the B&O's Mt. Clare depot, Benjamin H. Latrobe, Jr., Wendel Bollman, and Albert Fink, individuals equally well known to historians of civil engineering, were redesigning the American railroad truss bridge in iron. Hundreds of tons of cast- and wrought-iron bridge and enginehouse components were moving west by rail from Baltimore to be erected on the line then being built between Cumberland and Wheeling. Adjacent to the railroad's Mt. Clare foundry was

Ross Winans's locomotive works, and next door was the Hayward, Bartlett & Co. plant, which relocated there in 1850 and became Baltimore's major producer of architectural iron. (The historic exhibits at the B&O Railroad Museum at Mt. Clare contain wonderful examples of the mechanical and decorative uses of cast and wrought iron.)

In 1870, Maryland still ranked fifth among iron-producing states. A decade later, 2,000 workers manned more than fifty iron foundries in the Baltimore area, half a dozen of which made architectural castings. Baltimore's Poole and Hunt foundry furnished the iron columns for the dome of the U. S. Capitol in Washington and Hayward, Bartlett and Company, the iron door and window trim. The city's last working iron foundry, the Lacy Foundries in Fells Point, which started up during the Civil War as the Capitol was being finished, closed in 1989. It was not, however, an architectural ironworks.

The city and state were home to important manufacturers of iron long before the blast furnaces and coke ovens of Sparrows Point colored the night sky. Maryland's colonial iron industry was second only to

Pennsylvania's. The early ironworks, almost all of them charcoal fired, had aligned themselves along the three principal tiers of ore deposits: at the fall line near historic Route 1, where iron was mined from the 1700s almost until the First World War; in the Blue Ridge district; and far out in the Georges Creek coal basin of Western Maryland's Allegheny Plateau.

The first iron enterprise was a bloomery at North East, Maryland, at the head of the Chesapeake Bay, built prior to 1716. The Principio furnace, nearby, began operations in 1724. The previous year, Captain John Moale had viewed his furnace and ore bank at the mouth of the Gwynns Falls as more important than the founding of Baltimore—he delayed the laying out of the town and caused its site to be changed. Other early furnaces in the Baltimore area were at Elkridge (1759) and Northampton (1762). Pioneering ironworks fanned out north of Harpers Ferry in the Blue Ridge: Antietam, Mt. Etna, and Catoctin. Iron production in Western Maryland didn't begin until the 1820s and wasn't commercially feasible until the railroad arrived two decades later; Mt. Savage was its most important center.

The Abell Building, with a beautiful cast-iron storefront by Bartlett, Robbins & Co., still stands at Baltimore and Eutaw streets. Illus.: Howard's Monumental City.

Principio is probably the best known of the early ironworks. London capitalists dispatched John England to operate it in 1723. He found there a partly completed furnace, a short supply of ingredients to make iron, and a clerk, Stephen Onion, whom he fired for mismanagement. The workmen were drunken, ill-tempered ex-convicts or indentured servants. "You may assure yourselves that here hath been and is such ruin as I never saw," he wrote his British backers. England was not enamored of Maryland's weather, either, which he said was the "worst for fervours and coughs every fall successively. I should not have been willing to have sent a dogg of thine hither."[1]

The artisans at G. Krug and Son, 415 West Saratoga Street, have been creating practical and graceful iron products in Baltimore for 180 years, long enough to have restored some of the local work they originally produced. Blacksmith Andrew Schwatke shod horses and repaired farmers' wagons at this location in 1810, selling the business in 1841 to Andrew Merker, who later transferred it to Bavarian immigrant Gustav A. Krug. The current proprietor is the fifth-generation Krug to run the business; until fifty years ago, one had to speak German to work there. Some of the century-old coal forges and equipment are still in operation, but the wrought iron nowadays is steel.

But soon he had the furnace up and running. Principio supplied half the pig iron shipped to England prior to the Revolution. During the war, Principio, Antietam, and Mt. Etna provided cannon and balls to the Continental Army. Afterwards, the Principio furnace had an erratic career under American control until new owners, the Whitakers, took it over in 1836, and ran it for more than fifty years.

When John H. Alexander wrote his 1840 *Report on the Manufacture of Iron in Maryland*, he found a rebuilt furnace at Principio. It was shaped like an inverted flask, thirty-three feet high and eight feet wide at the boshes (the wider, lower part of the furnace), with a bellows powered by creek water. The ore came by ship from Baltimore, and oyster shells were used as flux. Principio was producing 1,100 tons of iron annually, all of which went to subsidiary forges in Elkton, where 150 workers turned it into sheet iron, boiler plate, and nails.

Alexander was one of the principals of the Georges Creek Coal and Iron Company, proprietors of the legendary company town of Lonaconing, Maryland. In 1839, their massive, fifty-foot-high sandstone furnace, which incorporated cast-iron beams and wrought-iron tie rods, was smelting seventy-five tons of iron a week using coke as fuel and on-site ore. The foundry cast machine parts, farm implements, stoves, hardware for locks for the Chesapeake and Ohio Canal, and the gates for a Baltimore insurance firm.

A few miles to the north, the Maryland and New York Iron and Coal Company had begun laying out its ironworks at Mt. Savage. Five years later, a visitor discovered a town of 2,000 people, a quarter of whom worked at two blast furnaces, several puddling furnaces, and an "immense rolling mill," making twenty-five to thirty tons of rails a day. The puddlers earned between three and five dollars a ton and during slow

Ornamental ironwork, G. Krug and Son.

times at the mill would take other jobs in the coal mines or on the Chesapeake and Ohio Canal rather than accept a cut in pay.

The company used some of their first product to lay a rail line to Cumberland, connecting the Mt. Savage works with the B&O Railroad. Philadelphia's Franklin Institute hailed the beginning of a new domestic manufacture and awarded their rails a silver medal. "Alleghany [sic] county, Maryland, is thus entitled to two of the highest honors in connection with the American iron trade," said a nineteenth-century industrial historian. "It built the first successful coke furnace and rolled the first heavy iron rails."[2]

The blast furnace at Lonaconing shut down in 1855, and the furnaces at Mt. Savage about ten years later; the rolling mill was dismantled in 1875, having been idle for many years. The production of pig iron at Principio was abandoned in 1891.

There were several reasons for the decline, including poor-quality iron ore in Western Maryland and obsolete furnaces. Railroads and canals reached the Great Lakes deposits after the Civil War; soon larger ironworks in Pennsylvania and Ohio were smelting great quantities of iron using the better and cheaper ore. Even during the good times, making iron was an enterprise of fluctuating profitability at best, dependent more on British prices and the domestic tariff than anything else. Maryland's annual production of pig iron remained stable from 1870 to 1880—roughly 54,000 tons—but in that decade the state fell from fifth highest to eleventh among the iron-producing states, and didn't recover until Sparrows Point started up in the late 1880s, using mainly Cuban ores.

But the biggest reason for Maryland's decline in iron production was steel. The Home Insurance Building in Chicago, designed by William Le Baron Jenney and built in 1885, was the first to employ Bessemer steel beams. It is now regarded as the archetypal modern, high-rise office building with a skeleton frame and curtain walls. By 1897, Sparrows Point was rolling steel rails commercially; like the iron T-rails of the 1840s, they had found their way into buildings. The advent of steel and the new construction techniques it inspired doomed the cast-iron front. The period between 1850 and 1900, roughly, as iron became steel and the typical downtown commercial building grew from five to twenty stories or higher, was its brief hour on stage.

There was also a Ruskinian reaction on the part of engineers and architects to the excesses of Victorian design, when iron was even used to imitate the branches of wood in rustic park benches. "Of all periods and styles of architecture which New York City has experienced," said a critic in 1891, "the cast-iron fronts were the most abhorrent."[3] But tastes change. A century later, Victoriana is collectible and iron-front buildings have been rediscovered as beautiful and important links with the past.

The introduction of iron as a primary structural material in the nineteenth century has been called the greatest single step in the history of civil engineering, because it freed both engineers and architects from their dependence on traditional wood and masonry and allowed them to experiment with new forms and combinations in bridges as well as buildings. The period of reliance on cast and wrought iron was the shortest for any major construction material, and the era of iron's influence one of the least understood.

We are still appreciating its importance in our twentieth-century lives in ways that might have pleased a B&O Railroad engineer who, in 1850 at the start of its ascendance, hailed iron as "essential to the success of mechanical practice in almost every department of art and science."[4]

NOTES

1. James M. Swank, *History of the Manufacture of Iron in All Ages,* etc., Philadelphia: 1884, p. 184; Earl Chapin May, *Principio to Wheeling,* New York: Harper and Brothers, 1945, p. 18.

2. Swank, ibid., pp. 196-97.

3. Louis De Coppet Berg, "Iron Construction in New York City," *The Architectural Record* 1 (July 1891-July 1892): 455.

4. William Parker, general superintendent, B&O Railroad Annual Report, 1850, p. 32.

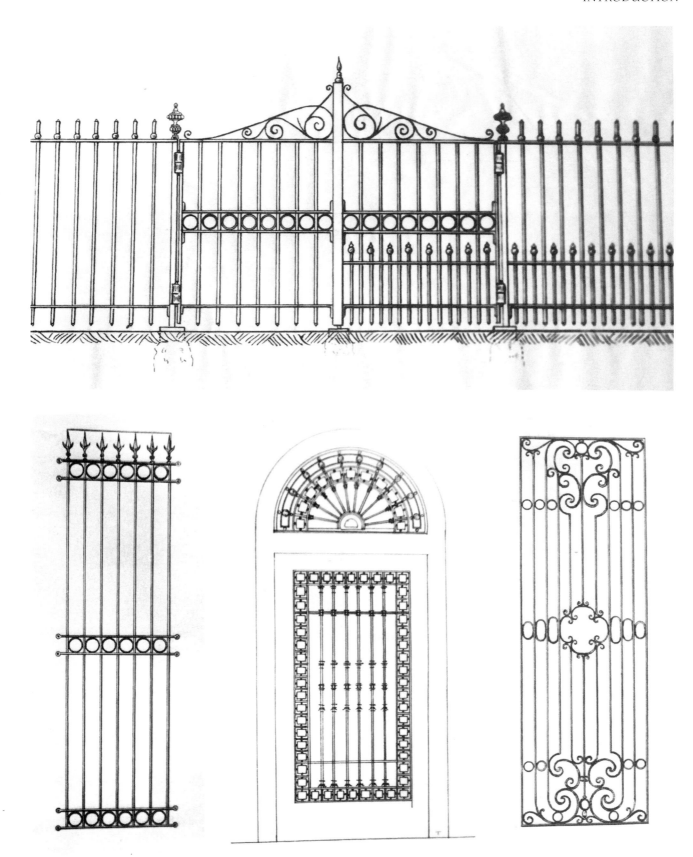

Many of the original drawings of fences, gates, transoms, and door guards still exist at G. Krug and Son and are used for new work and restorations.

Making use of old photographs, the Robinson Iron Corporation recreated a pair of two-story cast-iron porches for the Johns Hopkins Hospital's main building. Photo: James D. Dilts.

II. THE FOUNDER'S ART

by
J. Scott Howell

Baltimore's nineteenth-century iron-front buildings stand as a tribute to an age when designers preferred a material tough enough to withstand a harsh environment, fine enough to provide a medium of expression through intricate detailing, and cheap enough to be readily affordable.

Cast iron is a hard, brittle metal alloy composed primarily of three elements: iron, silicon, and carbon. Its brittleness is due to the relatively high percentages of the last two elements. Once a casting is made, its shape can be significantly altered only by the use of heavy-duty machine tools or abrasive grinders. This is in sharp contrast to more elastic alloys, like structural steel, which have only a trace of silicon and just one-seventh the amount of carbon found in a typical cast-iron alloy. Structural steel alloys can be bent or twisted with or without the application of heat.

Although cast iron's abundant carbon and silicon diminish its elasticity, these two elements are primarily responsible for its wonderful ability to withstand corrosion. When uncoated cast iron is exposed to the atmosphere, it begins to oxidize immediately. The process of rusting begins with a light reddish-brown hue, then progresses to a darker chocolate color as the surface of the metal becomes stable. Once this happens, the oxide layer protects the casting from further corrosion until it is removed. This is one of the main reasons for the continued existence, despite neglectful owners, of many century-old cast-iron facades. Founders purveying their products in the nineteenth century emphasized resistance to corrosion as a major benefit.

Cast iron can withstand heavy vertical loads, but is relatively weak in tension. For this reason, columns of cast iron can be made quite slender and delicate while horizontal beams must be more massive. The typical tensile strength of cast iron produced for architectural purposes is 25,000–30,000 pounds per square inch. Structural steel, by comparison, has more than double the tensile strength of cast iron. This was the primary reason that iron-front buildings were usually limited to five or six stories; if they went much higher, the cumulative weight became too great for the lower floor beams.

Cast iron is also quite heavy, weighing roughly four ounces per cubic inch, or approximately 430 pounds per cubic foot. (A cast-iron football would weigh more than 100 pounds.) This partly explains the reasons for thin-wall castings and relatively small components in architectural ironwork: Lighter material and smaller size meant less difficulty for the workmen who erected the components at the building site. Smaller castings were also less expensive and easier for foundries to produce, especially in mass quantities.

The methods of making architectural castings are essentially the same today as they were 100 years ago. Fine-grained molding sand mixed with a clay binder is packed around a pattern that looks exactly like the casting to be produced. After the mold is separated into two halves, the pattern is removed, leaving a

J. Scott Howell is vice president and general manager of Robinson Iron Corporation in Alexander City, Alabama. He has been actively involved in the iron restoration and custom casting business for over fifteen years in the United States and abroad.

hollow impression. When the two halves of the mold are put back together and clamped, the impression can be filled with molten iron poured through a hole, called a sprue, in the top half. After cooling, the casting is removed from the sand mold, cleaned, and machined if necessary before being used in its intended location.

The fabrication of these elaborate and precise architectural elements in the remarkably primitive surroundings of a nineteenth-century foundry resulted from the combined efforts of a variety of skilled craftsmen. The man who oversaw the whole operation was the *shop foreman*, whose word was law. He had extensive knowledge and experience of the molding and pouring process. Success or failure depended on his ability to provide clear leadership and a safe workplace, to demand performance, and to fabricate defect-free castings.

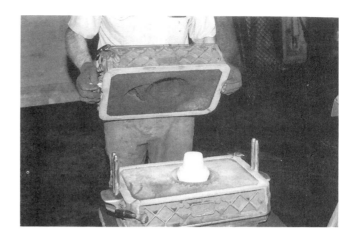

A typical sand mold is about to be closed prior to pouring. The core in the center of the mold will produce a hollow casting. Photo: J. Scott Howell.

A master pattern-maker at the Robinson Iron Corporation, Alexander City, Alabama, prepares a loose, working pattern. Photo: J. Scott Howell.

The *pattern-maker's* work was usually considered an art form, for he could take a drawing or sketch and turn it into reality. Working primarily in mahogany or white pine with hand tools, he understood the foundry process completely. For example, he made his patterns larger than exact size to account for the casting's shrinkage as the metal cooled in the mold (one-eighth inch per linear foot for cast iron). He made them thicker or heavier as their size increased. Greater thickness was necessary for larger patterns because the molten iron cooled quickly as it entered the sand mold and could solidify prematurely, resulting in a casting flaw commonly called a "cold shut." He knew how the metal flowed in the cavity, and provided the gate and runner system needed for success. He at-

tached this flow system to the pattern, forming a path through which the molten metal would travel as the mold was filled. Finally, and most importantly, he understood the concept of "draft," the angle on the edge of the pattern that allowed it to be lifted from the sand mold without tearing the mold wall. This edge forms what is known as the parting line of the pattern.

In the iron foundries of 100 years ago, the *molder* had to possess great strength and stamina. In a day's time he moved literally tons of molding sand from the floor to the mold forms, or flasks. He packed it tightly around the pattern with hand ramming tools and knew exactly how to lift the pattern and cut the sprue in the top half of the mold to make good castings. By feeling a handful of molding sand, he could tell if the

A white-hot stream of molten iron, tapped from the foundry cupola furnace at 2,700 degrees Fahrenheit, is transferred to a pouring bull, from which it will flow into sand molds to create architectural castings. Photo: J. Scott Howell.

moisture content was high or low, or if more clay binder was needed. He made sure the right amount of weight was placed on top of the mold so that the two mold halves would not separate during a pour, and worked closely with the pourer, tolerating nothing that might create a flaw in the casting. He was often temperamental, especially with regard to the patterns, and favored long production runs of the same one, which allowed him to eliminate the guesswork, produce more molds, and increase his piece-rate pay.

The *furnace-tender* had one of the most dangerous jobs in the old-time foundry. He layered 25 percent coal, 15 percent limestone, and 60 percent pig iron in the vertical cupola furnace, and operated the bellows to achieve the intense heat required to melt the iron at 2,700 degrees Fahrenheit. Lastly, he knew exactly when to tap the base of the furnace and allow the flow of molten iron to fill the pourers' ladles in order to reach the molds before loss of heat caused "dead iron," which had to be poured into pig beds for future use.

After cooling in the mold, the castings were shaken out and taken to the cleaning room, often called a

A foundryman tips molten iron from the pouring bull into a mold. After the casting hardens, it is shaken out, cleaned up, and machined for installation. Photo: J. Scott Howell.

scratch house in the early shops. Here the *grinder* removed the remaining molding sand with a wire brush and made free use of hammer and chisel to take off gates, runners, and the thin layer of iron called flashing that occurs at the parting line of the casting. For smaller items, he used a tumble mill: a large rotating drum filled with iron castings that cleaned themselves as they ground against one another.

The *machinist* drilled the mounting holes and provided the fitting necessary to put together a large cast-iron assembly—such as the facade of a building—from individual parts, and with his layout tools and templates insured a successful installation when the ensemble reached its destination.

The *inspector* was usually the shop owner or client, with the authority to reject castings that exhibited defects such as warpage, porosity, or cold shuts. These problems were common for architectural components with thin-wall sections or lacy decorative features. Such castings were difficult to produce unless the pouring temperature of the iron and the gating system were nearly perfect.

The nineteenth-century foundries, much like today's, preferred long, repetitive runs because they could achieve higher levels of production, lower costs, and a better product by making extensive use of a single pattern. Therefore, most of the larger foundries printed elaborate catalogs featuring their standard components, and invited architects or clients to pick and choose among them to create unique designs. This freedom, coupled with lower material costs, was very appealing to building professionals.

Cast iron was often used to imitate other building materials. Some of the earliest applications of cast iron replicated wrought-iron designs; many facades were made to look like cut stone, complete with quoining, Doric columns, bracketed cornices, and roof balustrades. Unlike stone, however, cast iron could be used in much thinner wall sections, reducing weight and foundation requirements and cutting costs. While cast iron weighs about two and a half times as much as granite, it has ten times the compressive strength.

Cast iron could also provide the designer with finer detailing than was possible with masonry. Great nineteenth-century architects such as Louis Sullivan were fascinated with the potential intricacy of iron castings and frequently commissioned original patternwork for their projects. Extensive use of classical Greek and Italianate ornamentation was quite common during the period.

Of the city's large-scale metal porches and balconies, once the pride of local foundries, only a few dozen remain. Most are in East Baltimore. This one, with its striking rinceau pattern, is at the rear of a restored apartment building, "The Convent," 1901-1911 East Lombard Street.

Finally, cast iron gave American builders something they especially cherished—speed. When properly manufactured and prefitted, a cast-iron facade took much less time to erect than traditional masonry. The years required for cut stone construction became mere months or even weeks with cast iron, and this feature also pleased building owners who could occupy their properties in less time.

The quantity and variety of iron facades erected in Baltimore and other American cities during the second half of the nineteenth century is astounding, especially considering the limitations under which the early construction crews operated. There were no cranes to lift heavy castings, no arc welders for joining one casting to the next, no electric drills to create missing bolt holes, and no portable air compressors for pneumatic grinding and painting in the field. But through information gained during iron-front restorations, and some imaginative reconstruction, we can surmise how it was done.

Like most construction, a typical iron facade began with a "footprint" or foundation plan. In many cases, the foundation was well below street level. Before steel-reinforced concrete, builders had to rely on heavy stones placed in undisturbed soil at the column

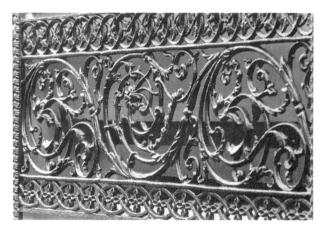

Detail, 1901-1911 East Lombard Street.

locations. These would have been carted in wagons to the site, loaded on timber skids with block and tackle, and dragged into place. A crew would then drill holes in the stones, one man holding and turning a star drill, or jumper, and the others swinging sledge hammers. Wrought-iron pins were inserted into the holes and molten lead poured around them; when the lead hardened, the cast-iron columns were attached to the pins and thus were supported by the stone foundation.

Usually round or square in shape and typically varying in wall thickness from one-half to one inch, these hollow columns were a special challenge to cast, because of the need to suspend a core horizontally in the sand mold to make the casting hollow. The core was also made of bonded sand and tended to float as

East Baltimore arabesque, the venerable two-level porch with an ornate grapevine motif on the northeast corner of Broadway and Lombard Street was recently restored by the owner.

Since it was shown in the Baltimore Sun *in 1953, wood has replaced two upper levels of metal on one of a matching pair of beautiful three-story cast-iron porches and stairways at the rear of 2221 and 2223 East Pratt Street.*

Detail, 2221 and 2223 East Pratt Street.

the molten iron entered the mold, causing warpage and voids in the casting. These problems, along with the weight factor, generally restricted column heights to fifteen feet or less.

After the columns were erected, they were topped with horizontal fascia (spandrel) beams that were usually wider than the diameter of the columns in order to withstand the load of the upper stories. Fascia beams were often cast-iron I-beams, spanning from column to column, and bolted to a plate at the top of each one. The material's relatively low tensile strength accounts for the short span between columns in the typical cast-iron facade.

The structural shape was almost always adorned with a decorative cornice casting featuring classical design motifs such as dentils or egg and dart molding, which was attached to the structural member through a system of wrought-iron bands or straps and bolts. These intermediate cornices on the cast-iron front were especially suited to signage featuring large, three-dimensional letters in gold leaf.

As the erection of the iron-front facade proceeded, floor by floor, a four- to six-man crew standing on heavy timber scaffolding used horse-drawn block-and-tackle rigging to hoist the castings, rarely weighing more than 1,000 pounds each, up to their intended levels. The workmen put together the individual pieces with screws, bolts, and backing plates, and attached the whole front by various means to what was usually a conventional wood and masonry structure behind it. Because the decorative elements were fragile, they were usually put on after the major structural members were erected. Thus, the acanthus leaves for a Corinthian column were almost always cast and attached separately with wrought-iron pins or flat-head screws.

The number of different patterns required for a typical five- to six-story iron front varied from 50 to 150 depending on the complexity of the design. These patterns were used repeatedly to create the building bays, and thousands of individual castings might go into a single facade. More repetition meant less labor and lower production costs, making iron-front construction significantly cheaper than intricately carved stone facades.

Small figures framed in a grapevine pattern and topped with a wire railing distinguish this unusual second-story porch at 136 South Patterson Park Avenue facing Pratt Street.

As iron-front technology expanded in the post-Civil War period, it gained greater public acceptance. The use of modular design and prefabrication improved the efficiency of the foundries and gave Americans a fast, economical way to develop their cities with a high level of aesthetics and design. With the growing popularity of the passenger elevator in the 1870s and the development of structural steel, the high-rise steel frame construction of the 1880s was a natural extension of iron-front building methods.

Once the iron facade was up, there was heavy use of lead-based paints and caulks, according to the evidence gathered to date. The original red lead primers were actually orange in color and were usually applied in thick layers to provide an effective shield from moisture penetration. A wide range of finish colors were used, but darker ones were preferred. There is no evidence to indicate any extensive use of paints on the interior surfaces of columns and cornice members. These were usually left to oxidize naturally through humidity and the inevitable leakage into the interior.

Detail, 136 South Patterson Park Avenue.

Water penetration and neglect are the biggest enemies of cast-iron facades. Although the metal protected itself with natural oxidation, the wrought-iron pins and bolts used by the construction crews deteriorated quickly when exposed, causing an eventual failure of the facade.

Along with architectural ironwork, nineteenth-century foundries took great pride in the diversity of their product lines. Cast iron had a wide range of domestic and commercial uses such as utensils, stoves, and steam-heating plants. Perhaps some of the most cherished pieces that came out of this period were site amenities: fountains, urns, furniture, and statuary. Many examples still exist in town squares and private gardens. A lot of this sculpture was actually made from a zinc-based alloy commonly called "pot metal." This material, and a wide variety of patterns, enabled the early foundrymen to make extensive use of lead-based solder to join multiple castings into complex sculptural shapes.

Cast iron is a time-tested building material, but it doesn't last forever. In nineteenth-century facades, the first evidence of deterioration is the loss of their attached ornamentation, typically at the column capital and cornice bracket locations. The outlook is promising, however, for long-term preservation.

The key to any job of this nature is an accurate assessment of the work, although concealed damage can make such an assignment difficult. The most appropriate procedure is to begin with a detailed photographic survey of the facade to determine the extent of the missing or damaged ornamentation. Dimensions are also necessary, allowing the contractor to perform the weight calculations for individual components, which can be a very important factor when a large number of new castings are required.

For large facades, an architect or qualified engineer should produce a clear, concise set of specifications, which would include the materials and restoration methods to be used. A competent foundry should then be called in to decide which individual facade components need to be replaced. The foundry can use the original castings as patterns by adjusting for the shrinkage factor and by refining the details with hand tools prior to molding and casting. The best available sample should be selected for pattern making because a new casting can never be as good as the pattern.

Cast iron's inherent hardness permits very abrasive cleaning methods. For shop cleaning, steel shot in a cabinet blaster is best. If enough of the metal is left, and is in reasonably sound condition, layers of paint and oxidation can be burned away with a torch prior to blasting. Since steel-shot blasting is not feasible for cleaning metal in situ, dry sandblasting is recommended. The cast iron will begin to oxidize immediately, so bare surfaces should be coated within forty-eight hours of cleaning.

Although cast iron is extremely difficult to weld, a strong bond can be obtained with a high-quality welding rod made of pure nickel. The process becomes even more difficult when attempting to make repairs on original material. In many cases, welding can worsen the situation. Repairing original iron with weldments should only be tried by experienced craftsmen. Welding is not appropriate for cracks in structural members. Structural cracking or severe deterioration around the attachment points are good reasons for recasting.

For dealing with small cracks and holes, a good epoxy steel is an excellent way to make cosmetic repairs, but the use of this material should be limited to nonstructural applications. Bonding is not a problem as long as it is applied over clean metal. In general, a casting should be replaced if the remaining wall section is less than three-eighths of an inch thick; however, this rule of thumb may not be applicable in all cases because the size of the casting and its load-bearing capacity determined its original wall thickness, which was sometimes less than that.

Baltimore's park pavilions also employed cast iron, usually as columns. In Union Square this "beautiful rotunda, supported by pillars of unique design," once covered a spring that supplied water to the nearby Mt. Clare depot of the B&O Railroad. The spring has been paved over and the elaborate cast-iron fence and gateways that surrounded the square have disappeared, but the 1851 rotunda remains. Photo: James D. Dilts.

The metal used today for newly cast material is officially known as Class 30 grey iron, ASTM A48. Alternative methods such as cast aluminum are not recommended for cast-iron facade restorations for two reasons. First, the introduction of another metal into an original iron facade can create galvanic corrosion. This occurs when, in the presence of moisture, the surface ions of one metal "borrow" from another of lesser "nobility," accelerating deterioration. Secondly, different metals tend to weather at different rates, creating an uneven appearance.

When no original exists or when the original is damaged beyond all hope, a new pattern must be carved. The pattern-maker often requires a full-scale drawing or layout to replicate the original accurately. Modern craftsmen use traditional wood, wax, and clay for their work as well as contemporary materials such as plastic urethane molding compounds. The cost of new patternwork is directly related to the intricacy and size of the design. The most difficult and expensive patterns usually involve high-relief ornamentation such as leaf moldings, medallions, and rosettes.

With new castings, the restored facade can be reassembled. Since welding to the original ironwork is difficult and messy, the preferred method is to use stainless steel fasteners which are commercially available in the same sizes used by the early foundries. In the reassembly phase, all the points of connection are scrutinized and strengthened with new fasteners and clip angles where possible.

Paint and coating systems have been greatly improved in recent years. Some of them offer excellent resistance to the extremely corrosive environments that exist in major East Coast cities with heavy automobile traffic. The best available paint system for cast iron is a two-part epoxy primer followed by a polyurethane finish coat. Unfortunately, these paints are quite expensive. For noncorrosive atmospheric conditions, a red-oxide alkyd primer followed by an alkyd enamel can be a more cost-effective finish. Areas of metal that will be concealed should be thoroughly primed prior to installation. Polyurethane caulks in tubes are recommended to prevent water penetration. A properly restored facade should last for at least as long as it existed prior to restoration.

Cast-iron-front buildings, fences, and balconies will undoubtedly continue to be objects of great sentiment and admiration for a growing segment of the American population, and the need to preserve them increases with each passing day. However, without governmental intervention or a significant reduction in preservation cost relative to the investment value of the property, many more structures will be lost.

George A. Frederick's Druid Hill Park pavilions, built in the 1860s and 1870s, are some of the oldest park structures in the country. His Chinese pavilion, shown here at Druid Hill and Fulton avenues, has fluted cast-iron columns with wooden brackets and fretwork. In 1994, it was moved across the street into the park proper and restored. Photo: James D. Dilts.

Technology can provide some solutions to the dilemma. Emerging foundry processes such as the evaporative polystyrene casting method are sweeping the industry. Here, a styrofoam pattern (replacing the historic wooden one) is placed in unbonded sand, and molten iron poured directly on it, turning the styrofoam into a gas which escapes through the sand particles. The iron takes the shape of the pattern with incredible accuracy. Through lasers and computer-aided design technology, the industry will soon be capable of carving these styrofoam patterns without using any traditional pattern-making methods. Thus, a pattern for a missing leaf detail could easily be generated by a three-dimensional model stored in a computer's memory.

This brings up an interesting question: How will we preserve the traditional skills and resources necessary for decorative and architectural casting work? Few of the old-time pattern-makers are left and many young people consider foundry work undesirable. Yet these things could change with more restoration projects and greater demand for skilled iron preservationists.

The octagonal Perkins Square cast-iron pavilion at George Street and Myrtle Avenue in West Baltimore, with neo-Grec details and a jaunty cupola and weathervane, dates from the 1870s. It formerly housed Perkins Spring and was surrounded by luxuriant beds of flowers arranged in intricate designs. Photo: James D. Dilts.

The permanence of cast iron appealed to stove founder A. Weiskittel, whose ironworks was located on Aliceanna Street in East Baltimore. The Weiskittel tomb in Loudon Park consists of flat plates scored to resemble ashlar, with pediment, piers, and scrolled side panels—all made of iron—painted in aluminum. The brick retaining walls and the steps are faced with iron as well. Photo: James D. Dilts.

The Hayward, Bartlett (later the Bartlett, Robbins) foundry cast numerous statues of "Sailor" and "Canton," Newfoundland dogs that became the firm's mascots (see the Bartlett, Robbins catalog, page 90). This is one half of the pair that still guard the Baltimore Gas and Electric Company's Spring Gardens plant in South Baltimore. Photo: James D. Dilts.

The Sun Iron Building as it appeared circa 1900 with two items added after its 1851 completion: the sunburst clock and the cupola. The iron-front building adjacent to the Sun (on the left in the photograph) was constructed the following year with castings supplied by one of the local foundries that worked on the Sun Iron Building. Photo: The Peale Museum, Baltimore City Life Museums.

III. THE SUN IRON BUILDING

by
David G. Wright

Construction of the Sun Iron Building in Baltimore, 1850-1851, represented a critical point in the acceptance of metal in urban architecture. For the first time, the all-iron structural and cladding principles of James Bogardus were applied to a project for an outside client. The huge iron-skeleton-framed and iron-faced commercial building, the largest such structure in the United States at its completion, would influence from that time forward not just Baltimore's downtown, but the downtowns of a majority of American cities.

In 1849, Arunah S. Abell, part owner and full proprietor of the Baltimore *Sun,* was one of the most successful and creative newspapermen in the country. Abell had learned the publishing trade in New York City in the early 1830s. With partners William Swain and Azariah Simmons, he founded the Philadelphia *Public Ledger* in 1836, and a year later moved to Baltimore to establish the penny *Sun.* Abell was one of the first to employ railroad, telegraph, and pony express to speed the collection of news, and he actively pursued the most advanced methods of typesetting and printing.

The desire to establish a new headquarters for the Baltimore publishing operation resulted from Abell's need for better printing equipment to accommodate increased circulation. The existing plant at the southeast corner of Baltimore and Gay streets was makeshift, not originally designed for the larger presses becoming available. Because of his earlier newspaper contacts, Abell must have been aware of the New York *Sun's* commitment to purchase two mammoth rotary presses invented by New Yorker Richard M. Hoe that could print an astounding 20,000 copies an hour. Two

similar presses would be installed in the new Baltimore building, and occupy much of the basement.

Abell had decided not simply to upgrade but, in the spirit of being at the head of the industry, to provide a model newspaper facility. A site worthy of this anticipated goal mandated the selection of land in the heart of the city, which was ultimately assembled on the southeast corner of Baltimore and South streets, consolidating five existing properties. The $50,000 necessary for the ground would rival the $2.20 per square foot required for the improvements. The total budget for the new building was over $100,000, more than twice the amount customary for urban construction at that time.[1]

During the planning period, probably in late 1849, the *Sun's* board of directors entertained a proposal from James A. Bogardus for the construction of a building with an iron structure and exterior iron cladding. Bogardus had been advocating these principles in New York for several years: a system that resisted fire, offered rapid erection, allowed large quantities of natural light to enter the interior, and even permitted dismantling and reconstruction elsewhere. Other than his own warehouse built in New York between 1847 and 1849, however, Bogardus had received no major commissions.[2] The calculated risk that the publisher took in accepting Bogardus was significant, but it proved as auspicious as Abell's other innovative deci-

David G. Wright is a principal of Grieves, Worrall, Wright, and O'Hatnick, Architects. Since the publication of his 1978 pamphlet, Baltimore City Cast Iron, *by New York's Friends of Cast Iron Architecture, he has continued to research Baltimore's cast-iron heritage.*

sions. Fires had been the constant scourge of all downtowns, and Abell undoubtedly saw a future where cities would be built with noncombustible materials.

Recognizing that the design of the exterior would be important to the building's success, Bogardus teamed up with New York architect Robert G. Hatfield. In 1850, Hatfield was thirty-four years old and headed a small design office at 23 Chambers Street, two blocks from Bogardus's operation. Hatfield brought to the project both expertise in the design manipulation of classical forms, and technical knowledge of construction.

The Sun commission launched Hatfield's career, as well as Bogardus's. Hatfield, who up to this point had designed residences and published a widely read manual on their detailing, became a significant influence in the New York architectural community. He was to be involved in the design of many commercial, institutional, and public buildings, with much of the work using iron, both as a facade element and as a structural component.[3] Best known may be his immense cast-iron arches that spanned New York's original Grand Central Depot, built in the early 1870s. When the American Institute of Architects was formed in 1857, Hatfield was elected treasurer, a post he held until his death in 1879. One of his most significant contributions to the profession—it received international acceptance—was his treatise on using iron as a structural material: *Theory of Transverse Strain.* This work had its seeds in the design and erection of the Baltimore project.

Precise design dates for the Sun Iron Building must be inferred, as no construction drawings have yet surfaced. The overall arrangement of interior space was still unsettled when ground was broken on April 1, 1850. There were plans to incorporate a steam-operated elevator, but they were later dropped, perhaps due to the questionable track record of the invention. Otis's safety catch was two years in the future.

However, the foundations for the project were set, and they extended roughly twenty-three feet beyond the property line along both Baltimore and South streets to gain more underground area for the printing presses. This technique of incorporating adjacent public property, familiar in New York, marked a significant first for Baltimore. A recently approved municipal ordinance, advocated by the *Sun*'s proprietors, provided that two-fifths of the street's width could be captured for underground use. For the *Sun*, this meant a gain of an amazing 80 percent in the building's basement floor plate, for which the owner was sub-

The new underground pressroom of the New York Sun, *equipped with Richard M. Hoe's rotary presses and lit by Thaddeus Hyatt's patented sidewalk vault lights, was pictured in the* Scientific American *in 1851. The Baltimore* Sun's *pressroom, under construction at the same time, had a similar appearance. Illus.: Enoch Pratt Free Library, Baltimore.*

jected to a $600 surcharge. The gain for Abell was clearly worth the cost.

The hole being dug between April and July 1850, to the unusual depth of seventeen feet, disrupted traffic on the busy thoroughfares, and did not go unreported. In a brief article, the first concerning its future home, the *Sun* joked about workmen digging for gold, but acknowledged that the excavation was considerable.[4]

To create the sidewalk above this extended subterranean area, the designers used a series of cast-iron plates containing small disks of thick glass. Thaddeus Hyatt of New York had patented these vault lights in 1845 and used them there. For Baltimore, however, this also was a novelty. The dense glass allowed natural light to filter into the pressrooms, generically depicted in *Scientific American* in 1851.[5]

To ventilate the basement, an ingenious system of hollow iron posts with perforations at their tops extended up through the sidewalk at the edge of the street. Architecturally, the posts held awnings to shade both the storefronts and the sidewalk, but for the printing rooms these decorative cast pipes provided fresh air. To the pedestrian, the awning posts offered an olfactory awareness of the processes going on below: "[The] delightful smell of printer's ink and steam . . . arose through the iron," said a more recent chronicler.[6] The basement granite piers formed a structural grid of square units 18 feet on a side. Their construction, with the brick vaults and retaining walls, which were parged with clay as a waterproofing measure, continued into the fall of 1850.

The superstructure of iron appeared during the winter and early spring of 1851. The above-ground building measured fifty-six feet along Baltimore Street and seventy four feet along South, with a five-story height of seventy feet. The interior grid of cast-iron columns supported arched cast-iron beams. The building at the time of its construction was the tallest completely iron-framed commercial structure in America.

The Sun Iron Building faced the offices of its competitor, the Baltimore American, across South Street after the latter built a new building in 1876 with an ornate cast-iron front furnished by Bartlett, Robbins & Co. The view, taken in the late 1870s, looks west on Baltimore Street. Photo: Ross J. Kelbaugh Collection.

The only earlier example was Bogardus's own three-story factory. Paxton's Crystal Palace in London, built simultaneously, was certainly more expansive, but contained only three stories with a total height of sixty-four feet.

Analyzing the construction of the Sun Iron Building's flooring system requires careful consideration. Bogardus's patent, approved May 7, 1850 (and certainly developed before he and Hatfield finalized the structural designs and detailing for Abell), contained a description of iron flooring. Narrow iron plates, sharply corrugated to provide strength in spanning, would be placed upon the iron beams and would interlock with their neighbors. In his writings, Bogardus claimed that his factory in New York had been built according to this patent, but historians have raised questions as to whether he used wood joists between his iron beams to support the iron flooring. When the factory was dismantled in 1859, contemporary news reports mentioned "timbers" being removed.[7]

The Sun Iron Building remains a similar enigma, with current research indicating a less-than-total iron flooring system. Wood spanned structurally over the metal beams. On top of the plank, ridged sheets of iron were laid to provide what Bogardus felt was a fire separation between floors. This was topped with a layer of cement to supply additional fire protection and, indirectly, more compressive strength, as well as to create a level platform for the wooden flooring. In execution, this was a forerunner of what is commonly known today as a corrugated metal deck and concrete flooring system. Perhaps unsure of the load-carrying capacity of the metal deck system, Bogardus chose to reinforce it with the timber underneath. These uncertainties, however, do not diminish the general significance of this major, skeletal frame structure that later designers emulated and developed.

The Baltimore foundry of Adam Denmead and Sons manufactured the exterior ventilating awning posts and most of the interior structural iron, to the chagrin of Bogardus, who probably would have preferred to control this process in New York. (Although Bogardus personally had no foundry, he was surrounded by three capable ones.) The reason for employing the Baltimore firm stems from Abell's original agreement with Bogardus, which required that all production, exclusive of proprietary or patented items, remain local.[8] This involvement gave Baltimore foundries an early and important exposure to what would emerge as a major industry.

Between "Brown's Building, 1860" (right foreground) and the amazing Methodist Book Depository's five-story cast-iron facade created by an unknown foundry (shown in a front view opposite) is James Bogardus's 1852 iron front for Samuel Shoemaker. The location is the north side of Baltimore Street between Calvert and St. Paul streets. Circa 1878 photo: Ross J. Kelbaugh Collection.

Denmead's Monumental Foundry, established in 1840 at the corner of North and Monument streets, developed into one of the city's major casting plants. It produced locomotives and cars for Baltimore's three railroads, and manufactured equipment for local industries that processed cloth, flour, sugar, tobacco, and lumber. Structural iron pieces for bridges and mill castings were available from Denmead as early as 1845. In late 1850, the firm supplied thirty-three-foot-wide, ground-floor front and rear facades for the new showrooms and factory of carriage maker William McCann at 35 South Gay Street, perhaps the first such building in Baltimore. Later architectural iron by Denmead included the first-story front for the liquor warehouse of William T. Walters in January 1852, and in November, the storefront at 107 Baltimore Street, adjacent to the Sun Iron Building, first occupied by silk merchant W. King. Denmead's major focus, how-

ever, remained the locomotive and metal-clad shipbuilding industries, leaving much of the architectural iron casting to others who would specialize in that field.

The exterior ironwork of the Sun Building appeared in early spring, 1851. Hatfield's design called for expansive ground-floor display windows on both primary elevations to be protected with rolling iron shutters. Daniel D. Badger of New York, who operated a foundry within earshot of Bogardus, had developed the storefront, securing patents for the shutter from Baltimore inventor Arthur L. Johnston in 1843, and manufacturing all the components. He became a major competitor to Bogardus in the development and dispersal of cast-iron construction. The Sun Iron Building was the first time these two giants worked together, an important development for both.

The remainder of the exterior design for the Sun Iron Building differed significantly from all previous cast-iron projects. Architecturally, it signaled the beginning of the iron-front era. The precedents did exist, but the material's ability to express sculptural detail was yet to be manifested. John Haviland's 1829 design for the front of the Pottsville, Pennsylvania, bank, one of America's first iron fronts, used flat plates to imitate stone. Bogardus's earlier works in New York, for the Milhau drugstore, the Laing Building, and his own factory, were all of a similar, decidedly two-dimensional design.

For the Sun Iron Building, perhaps with the enthusiasm of Bogardus to encourage him, Hatfield produced four vigorous upper stories, grouped visually into two paired stages. Applied piers at the second, third, and fourth stories formed a base at the fifth to support twenty-three life-size statues, modeled on Washington, Franklin, and Jefferson. Cast-iron bas-relief images of Washington and Franklin ornamented the three sides of each second-story pier pedestal. The projecting and ornamented top cornice was supported with scroll brackets at each bay. Pier capitals at all levels displayed a blending of the Ionic and Corinthian orders. All of the exterior iron was originally painted a bronze color that offered a rich metallic appearance—unlike several contemporary iron fronts that strove to simulate stone, the Sun flaunted its metal. This exuberant, almost baroque assemblage of pieces to create depth, interest, and verticality, modeled the form and character of cast-iron fronts for the next twenty to thirty years.

Significantly innovative, the entire front as an ensemble received some early criticism: The design of the first story was not visually strong enough to carry the panoply occurring overhead. The *Sun*'s own account rationalized the design, indicating that the first-story openings, for business economy, had to be as generous as possible.[9] Critic Turpin Bannister was less kind, simply noting that Badger's first-floor storefronts formed a curiously weak base for the activity above. It is not known who had charge of the original design of the facade. With the three strong personalities of Bogardus, Badger, and Hatfield all present, it seems clear that each contributed portions, but that no one individual was in total control.

Baltimore's Benjamin S. Benson fabricated all of the upper-story exterior cast iron. A machinist trained in Ross Winans's locomotive shops, Benson was new on the scene as an independent foundryman. The Sun project was his first architectural work in cast iron, but he quickly followed it with others, including a sixty-one-foot-wide front and rear first-story facade for merchants Brooks, Lilly, and Carter on West Baltimore Street in 1852. (A portion of the rear elevation of this building still stands at 318 West Redwood Street; it is the city's oldest cast-iron storefront.) Benson remained active in the architectural casting business for more than a decade, later expanding into the manufacture of railroad cars and gas pipe.

Benson's participation in the Sun project may well have been due to his involvement with the reestablished Maryland Institute for the Promotion of the Mechanic Arts. This association of inventors, scientists, and manufacturers, based loosely on the Franklin Institute in Philadelphia, had been formed in 1826, but disbanded after a disastrous fire in 1835. In 1847, Benson, aged 30, was instrumental in its reorganization,

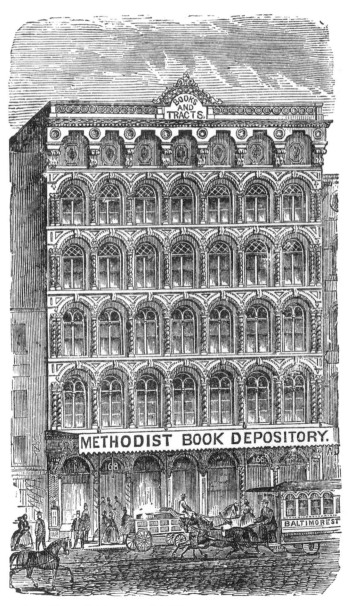

Illus.: Howard's Monumental City.

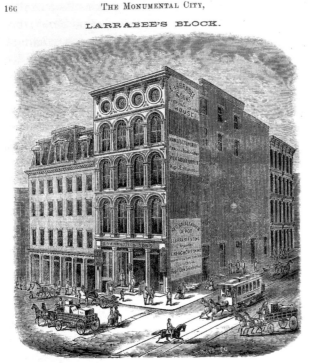

LARRABEE'S BLOCK.

E. LARRABEE & SONS,
WHOLESALE
LEATHER
AND
SHOE FINDINGS,
NO. 20 S. CALVERT STREET,
BALTIMORE.

Bogardus used the same design for his other Baltimore building, erected in 1853 on South Calvert Street. Neither of the local structures by the inventor of the cast-iron front still exists. Illus.: Howard's Monumental City.

and Adam Denmead was elected vice-president. Benson and Denmead served on various committees and both became life members.

Other institute members included William McCann and William H. Reasin. The latter, a young architect originally from Aberdeen, Maryland, and a teacher at the institute, had designed the former's iron-front warehouse (for which Denmead supplied the castings). Reasin was also selected to design the institute's new headquarters, which were under construction during the same period as the Sun project. The institute building contained his cast-iron library fabricated by Benson.[10]

Abell chose Reasin to work with Bogardus and Hatfield as the designer for the interior of the Sun Iron

Building. After its completion, Reasin located his architectural practice on the second floor and remained there for over a decade. He later worked directly with Bogardus as architect for Bogardus's two other Baltimore projects. The first, completed in August 1852, was for Samuel Shoemaker, local superintendent of the Adams Express Company. Located at 164 West Baltimore Street, it was three bays wide and five stories high. The second, at 20 South Calvert Street, was for Ephraim Larrabee, wholesale leather merchant. It opened in April 1853 and, although four bays wide, used the same castings.[11] Shoemaker and Larrabee were also members of the Maryland Institute, whose role in the acceptance and advancement of cast-iron architecture in Baltimore was great.

The interior of the Sun Iron Building, completed by the late summer of 1851, provided space for rental income as well as for the needs of the newspaper. The entire ground floor except for the public business office of the *Sun*, held commercial shops. The first occupants were a book publisher, a hatter, and a coal agent. The publisher, Burgess, Taylor and Company, was the marketing agent for *Gleason's Pictorial* of Boston, which wrote a glowing account of the building upon its completion. Joshua Vansant, a major force in the early leadership of the Maryland Institute, owned the hat store. The coal agent, Charles West, relocated within a year to his own newly constructed cast-iron building on Baltimore Street near Gay, designed by Reasin.[12]

Three separate telegraph companies leased much of the Sun Building's second floor and created the country's first communications center integrated with a newspaper operation. Their presence resulted in the maze of telegraph poles lining Baltimore Street thereafter. The remainder of the second floor accommodated offices for lease and a public meeting room used for the newly organized Merchant's Exchange, a clearinghouse for information concerning construction contracts being let within the city. The paper itself occupied the upper three levels: composing and editorial departments on the third and fourth floors and the type and stereotype foundry on the fifth. Tenants started moving into the building in August 1851, and the *Sun* officially began publication there on Saturday, September 13, 1851.

The Sun Iron Building opened to considerable local praise. The Baltimore *American* published the first complete account of the construction history two weeks after occupancy and complimented their neighbor on the architectural elegance and business convenience of the new headquarters. Boston's *Gleason's Pictorial* wrote

28

two weeks later that the building represented one of the most embellished they had encountered, and indicated that its fame already extended to Europe. The *Sun* maintained a discreet silence. Their mid-construction update, published in August 1850, was copied verbatim from an article in the *American*. When the *Sun* finally gave its readers a front-page engraving and history of the project, a full nine months after occupancy, it chose to para-phrase, almost in its entirety, the *Gleason's Pictorial* account.[13]

The building generated immediate tourist interest. In 1852, the locally published *Stranger's Guide to Baltimore* dedicated two pages and a full engraving to its description. Similar information and graphics were published in other guide books for over twenty years. Fifteen years after its completion, William Preston of the Maryland Institute recognized its effect anew, saying, "it stands in its architectural beauty and utility a lasting memorial to quiet integrity, liberal enterprise, and persevering industry."[14]

The Sun Iron Building had a major impact on the local development of cast-iron architecture. Within eighteen months of the building's completion, the city boasted seventeen partial and five full cast-iron-front commercial buildings. Seven had partial or total interior cast-iron structural framing. Of the group, Benson had cast three, and Denmead, four. However, another emerging Baltimore firm, Hayward, Bartlett & Co., was already in the lead with six architectural iron projects completed. This firm had provided the heating plant for the Sun project. Ultimately, Hayward, Bartlett would become one of the largest and most respected foundries in the country producing architectural cast iron. They shipped facades and entire structures to all areas of the United States and even abroad. In 1872, Horace Greeley referred to them as "one of the largest and best established architectural works in the United States."[15]

The firm's history dated to 1837 when Jonas Hayward arrived in Baltimore from Milford, New Hampshire, and set up shop marketing cast-iron stoves on Light Street, opposite Mercer. By coincidence, the first offices of Abell's penny *Sun* were located in the same building, on adjacent floors. Hayward and his several early partners originally bought their iron parts already cast. Not until 1849, after entering partnership with David L. Bartlett, did Hayward obtain foundry capabilities.

Originally from Hartford, Connecticut, Bartlett had established a stove business in Baltimore in 1844, and then opened a foundry, first on President Street, close to Benson's, and later on Leadenhall Street. In 1850, the firm's specialties were still stoves and cast-iron pipe. Buildings were just beginning to receive indoor plumbing as we know it today, in conjunction with hot water or steam heating supplied by remote furnaces. Hayward and Bartlett placed themselves at the head of this field and thus were the logical choice for doing that work on Abell's Sun Building. In the process, they must have recognized the possibilities in expanding their market to include architectural cast iron.

In 1850, while Benson and Denmead were producing castings for the Sun project, Hayward and Bartlett decided to relocate Bartlett's foundry once more, this time to a huge new 160- by 170-foot, three-story facility of their own design, located at the corner of Scott and Pratt streets, adjacent to Ross Winans's massive locomotive works.[16] Already, they employed over 150 men in the manufacture of castings. The descendants of Hayward, Bartlett & Co. would eventually take over Winans's plant, and remain in the iron business at this combined location for over 120 years.

In 1851, to reinforce the firm's early commitment to this new branch of work, they were involved with a rebuilding of their own downtown showroom, still at Light and Mercer streets, but at that point shared with property owner William Russell who manufactured and sold glass bottles. Two months after the Sun Iron Building opened, this thirty- by fifty-seven-foot showroom and warehouse was completed, with a first-story ornamental iron front containing thirteen-foot Ionic columns. All the floors were supported by interior fluted cast-iron columns.[17]

The influence and significance of the Sun Iron Building outside Baltimore was even greater than its local impact. Within four years, its principles of iron framing, with improvements, and its singular iron facade, re-emerged in the important Harper and Brothers book publishing headquarters in New York.

Harper and Brothers had suffered a disastrous fire on December 10, 1853, and chose to rebuild with fire-proof construction, seeking state-of-the-art technology. Again Bogardus was selected to participate, but the architect this time was John B. Corlies. The interior iron frame used beams of wrought iron (rather than cast), for added tensile strength; and the floor timbers were eliminated in favor of shallow brick vaults, but the concept was one of a clear iron skeleton similar to that of the Sun Iron Building.

The iron front of the Harper and Brothers Building matched exactly the design of the Sun Building in

Baltimore, even down to the cast statues at the fifth level. By 1854, Bogardus had patterns for several buildings that were capable of duplication, but Abell's project was the one Harper and Brothers permitted Corlies and Bogardus to select. Hayward, Bartlett & Co. cast the front for the Harper project and shipped it to New York in 1854. How and why control of the patterns shifted from Benson to Hayward, Bartlett & Co. remains a mystery, but a reasonable assumption is that Bogardus accepted proposals from any number of local Baltimore foundries to reproduce the castings, and Hayward, Bartlett provided the low bid. The Harper and Brothers Building has been mistakenly recognized as the country's first large commercial cast-iron building.[18] Clearly, the Sun Iron Building, its predecessor by four years and the source of its design, more appropriately deserves the title.

The duplication of the Sun Building facade was not limited to the Harper Building. Numerous additional Bogardus commissions displayed varying amounts of the patterns. The building at 254-260 Canal Street in New York, constructed in 1857, still stands as a five-story corner property with striking similarities, particularly in the pier details, and in the second- and third-story window arrangements.[19] In Philadelphia the same year, Bogardus erected for William Swain, Abell's newspaper partner, a speculative rental building of seven bays, five stories high, with about 90 percent duplication of the patterns, including the decorative pier medallions of Washington and Franklin, and the fifth-story iron statues.[20] Here, the representations of Washington and Franklin were joined by Johann Faust and Johannes Gutenberg. Two other more humble New York properties used the Washington and Franklin medallions and may well be attributed to Bogardus.[21]

The Sun Iron Building did much to make cast iron acceptable in the building industry, and to spread the fame of Bogardus as one of its primary advocates. One wonders why the building has not been appropriately acknowledged in the recent literature. Foremost among the reasons may be the *Sun's* reticence concerning its own enterprise. Whereas Abell relied on others to describe the achievement, his emulators, particu-

By 1854, Baltimore's Hayward, Bartlett & Co., begun as a stoveworks, had become an architectural foundry that duplicated the castings from the Sun Iron Building and shipped them to New York for erection as the Harper and Brothers Building, 331 Pearl Street. Circa 1880–1885 photo: Brown Brothers.

Another Manhattan building that drew on the design of the Sun Iron Building for inspiration was Bogardus's 1857 structure at 254-260 Canal Street. Photo: Becket Logan.

Bogardus designed a speculative property in Philadelphia for A. S. Abell's newspaper partner William Swain, using almost all of the Sun Iron Building patterns. It is no longer standing. Photo: Rare Book Department, Free Library of Philadelphia.

larly Harper and Brothers, extolled their own efforts. Bogardus, a promoter who initially relied heavily on his Baltimore achievement, needed little reference to it once the Harper Building was complete. In fact, because other foundries quickly realized that the process of casting and erecting iron-framed buildings and fronts was not necessarily proprietary, competition with Bogardus from the Baltimore community was great.

Lastly, the building proved to be less fireproof than its original promoters anticipated. Like steel, when cast iron is exposed to intense heat, its structural properties diminish. Only by applying fireproof insulation, common now with all metal frame construction, can the material be properly protected. When Baltimore suffered its terrible fire of February 7-8, 1904, the Sun Iron Building, lacking structural insulation, was destroyed, along with over forty-two square blocks of downtown stone, brick, cast-iron, and wooden commercial and industrial buildings. George W. Abell, son of the founder and then editor of the paper, stayed in the building until forced out at midnight, when "sparks began raining down like hail. Then the windows blew out. The building seemed to lift off the ground, and soon the walls caved in . . ."[22] With the city's attempt to forget the tragedy of the fire, together with efforts to rebuild, the "old" Baltimore character and history were put aside.

Awning posts, brick bearing walls, structural columns, and the blackened clock were all that remained of the Sun Iron Building in this photograph taken after the great Baltimore fire of February 7-8, 1904. Shortly before midnight February 7, publisher A. S. Abell was one of the last to leave the building, reported H. L. Mencken in The Sunpapers of Baltimore: *"[Then] some of the upstairs windows blew out, and in twenty minutes the heavy linotype machines on the fifth floor were falling though the blazing editorial and counting-rooms to the pressroom in the cellar . . . and that was the melancholy end of one of old-time Baltimore's most famous landmarks." Photo: Maryland Historical Society, Baltimore.*

The Sun Iron Building deserves a rediscovery and renewed appreciation. The casting firms and the architects who were involved with the undertaking all played significant roles in the development and use of iron throughout Baltimore and the entire country.

NOTES

1. Two other contemporary downtown warehouse–commercial properties were being built for about ninety cents per square foot: the Walters property at the Exchange (Baltimore *Argus,* 14 January 1852); and the Bonn Brothers property (Baltimore *Sun,* 15 February 1851).

2. Bogardus's career has been documented in several journals, but the definitive account is still necessary. See Turpin Bannister, "Bogardus Revisited," *Journal of the Society of Architectural Historians* 15 (December 1956): 4; and 16 (March 1957): 1, for an excellent background discussion.

3. Together with Daniel Badger, Hatfield designed six iron-front stores on Broadway in New York, including one for Tiffany and Company. See Daniel Badger, *Illustrations of Iron Architecture,* 1865, republished New York: Da Capo Press, 1970; and Dover Publications, 1981.

4. *Sun,* 28 June 1850.

5. *Scientific American* 6 (24 May 1851): 283. The article also mentions the installation of the rotary press in the New York *Sun's* property between 1849 and 1851.

6. Letitia Stockett, *Baltimore, A Not Too Serious History,* Baltimore: 1936, p. 91.

7. For a detailed description of Bogardus's factory and its dismantling, see Bannister, "Bogardus Revisited."

8. F. A. Richardson and W. A. Bennett, editors, *Baltimore: Past and Present,* Baltimore: 1871, p. 34.

9. 24 April 1852.

10. For an excellent account of the institute project, see Baltimore *Patriot and Commercial Gazette,* 13 October 1851.

11. *Sun,* 28 August 1852; Baltimore *American,* 23 April 1853.

12. *Sun,* 2 October 1852.

13. *Gleason's Pictorial* 1 (4 October 1851): 356-57; *Sun,* 26 August 1850, 24 April 1852.

14. Richardson and Bennett, *Baltimore, Past and Present,* p. 158.

15. Horace Greeley, et al., *The Great Industries of the United States,* Hartford: 1872, p. 512.

16. *Sun,* 10 July 1851.

17. *Sun,* 14 November 1851.

18. For example, see Carl Condit, *American Building,* Chicago: University of Chicago Press, 1982, p. 83.

19. *Society for Industrial Archeology Newsletter* 14 (1985): 13.

20. Casper Souder, Jr., *The History of Chestnut Street.* File at the Free Library of Philadelphia, Rare Book Department. The library owns four statues from the building. Photographs of them appeared in *Sculpture of a City: Philadelphia's Treasures,* Franklin Park Association, 1974, p. 64.

21. The Ahrenfeldt China Store on Murray Street (now demolished), and 63 Nassau Street; Gayle and Gillon, *Cast-Iron Architecture in New York,* pp. xiii, 2-3.

22. Eyewitness account by Walter A. Poole, *Sun,* 24 December 1950.

Passing through a small doorway and emerging suddenly into a large open space (a Renaissance device), the visitor is surrounded by six full floors of books. The stack room of the Peabody Library is a symphony in metal. Its lectures, art exhibits, and collections made the library for many years the center of intellectual life in the city. The stately columns, with their classical embellishments in gold leaf, are regal, and to labor in this ethereal space, where Mencken researched The American Language *and John dos Passos wrote his later works, is serious and sobering business. Shakespeare may have described it best: "the quick forge and working house of thought . . ."*

Two bays of the stack room illustrate the precision and symmetry of the neo-Grec style, which is closely associated with metal construction.

IV. THE PEABODY LIBRARY

by
Phoebe B. Stanton

The Peabody buildings exemplify the response of the nineteenth century when it confronted, thanks to the Industrial Revolution, nontraditional building materials and methods of construction. The Peabody Institute, 1859–1866, at the southeast corner of the Washington Monument, and the library to its east, 1876–1878, also typify the architectural tastes and requirements of Baltimore gentlemen of those years.

Before Americans faced the problems raised by the arrival of new ways of building and new materials, two parties in Europe had already come to grips with the question of whether to accept and how to employ these new techniques. Some clients, architects, and critics were convinced that architecture should cleave to the historic styles—Gothic or classical were those most used—and that buildings and the talents of their designers ought to be appraised according to the extent that they achieved the impossible—eclectic accuracy. These were often political conservatives who also refused to acknowledge that a new age, accompanied by fresh political needs as well as a new kind and style of building, had arrived. Relating the historical styles to an idealized view of the political, religious, and social virtues of the time that had first produced them, they insisted that revival of the style of an admired historic period could play a part in reform of society in their own time. In 1831, in *The Spirit of the Age* (essays written for *The Examiner*), John Stuart Mill described those who held such views as "men who carry their eyes in the back of their heads and can see no other portion of the destined track of humanity than that which it has already travelled." In 1872 the anony-

mous writer who dealt with the subject of architectural ironwork in Horace Greeley's *The Great Industries of the United States* pointed to John Ruskin as a writer who objected "to iron in architecture for sentimental reasons."

A second party, as far to the left as the other was to the right, was linked to liberal ideas. It declared that a new age demanding architectural design responsive to its needs had been born, that new building materials and techniques would create a modern architectural style as characteristic of the nineteenth century as Gothic and classical had been of theirs, and that, rather than the works of architects, the bridges, canals, tunnels and even factory buildings being created by engineers were the significant modern monuments. Thoughts of this kind were being expressed in Germany as early as 1835, when a critic announced, "Intimately acquainted as we are now become with the properties of every kind of material, whether wood, metal, or artificial substitutes for stone, and with the laws of statics in respect to them, we possess the means of providing whatever we require," and called for an inventive architecture "unfettered by formal

Phoebe B. Stanton is Professor Emerita of Art History, the John Hopkins University.

The author is indebted to Elizabeth Schaaf, archivist, the Peabody Institute, to John W. McNair, who has studied the hundreds of surviving drawings for the buildings of the institute, to the remarkable collection of books in the Peabody Library, for it contains extraordinary materials on architecture and the building arts, and, finally, to the buildings themselves, which are a continuous joy and source of inspiration.

precedents." In 1837 an English commentator on architecture looked to the United States, where there were no powerful stylistic precedents, to create "an entirely new and independent style of architecture" that would "accommodate itself to all the exigencies of a community."[1]

The contrast between these two positions raised issues larger than the dilemma of the styles. It suggested that, with the employment of prefabrication, construction could become less labor intensive because parts of structures were standardized and manufactured repetitively; that the many large buildings and engineering projects required to serve the new age would encourage the development and use of innovative building methods; and that the introduction of iron could lead to a new aesthetic.

But most architects and their clients—the builders of the Peabody were among them—took a position midway between these parties. They wanted the economy and efficiency of metal construction, yet they were unwilling to forsake the associational pleasures and ornament of the historical styles. No building is more typical of this response than the Houses of Parliament in London, begun in 1836 and completed in the 1860s. A masterpiece of revived Gothic, it was, beneath its ornament, a functional building of the new age, equipped with an elaborate system of mechanical ventilation and walls and floors of iron and tile designed to be as fireproof as advanced architectural technology could make it.

Inexorable social and economic pressures and innovations led to the development of prefabrication. The expansion of the dominion of Europe in the nineteenth century and improvements in transportation caused movements of people and the need for shelter in distant places. Industry responded with dwellings that could travel, "knocked down," with their owners to Australia, South America, and San Francisco to be assembled at their destinations without specialized labor. Such buildings were responsive to need rather than to disagreements about the meaning of the historic styles. Today we know that prefabrication of this kind was one manifestation of the process that led to widespread use of cast iron in building, that it foreshadowed methods of construction that prevail in the twentieth century, and that it brought stylistic changes in architectural design. Gilbert Herbert, in his study *The History of Prefabrication*, says that "this transfer from ad hoc building to planned multiple production is one of the fascinating break points in the curve of architectural evolution."

In the 1840s Baltimore was a thriving industrial community, shipbuilding center, and port from which people departed for California and South America. Eighteen forty-nine was the year of what were called "California houses" produced by both American and English industrialists. At least four manufacturers in Baltimore—B. S. Benson, Lapouraille and Mauglin, Rhoads, and McComas—were building prefabricated structures with cast-iron frames into which precut wooden walls and windows fitted, that could be assembled when they reached their destinations.[2] The city was also endowed with inventors and iron founders—Denmead, Poole and Ferguson, Murray and Hazlehurst, Millholland, and Hayward and Bartlett (the last would figure in the construction of the Peabody buildings)—who designed and manufactured iron castings of various kinds.[3] Baltimore, for example, required bridges to join the parts of the town as it developed, materials to supply the burgeoning railroad industry, and castings for ships. The Baltimore *Sun* on July 28, 1848, could report that "the Baltimore iron business in castings is equal to any."

Cast iron for architectural purposes was both structural and decorative. It could replace wooden beams and trusses in the support of roofs, and masonry in the construction of walls; its rigidity and capacity to bear loads meant that an iron frame of relatively slender dimensions could replace larger supports and so open up exterior walls and interior spaces. It also made decoration cheap. A carved wooden pattern was required, and once it was prepared, a sand mold in which the image of the pattern was impressed could be used repeatedly to receive molten metal. If the casting was to be thin, wax of the desired thickness was laid between the mold and a fireproof core. When the wax was removed, the mold and core were fixed in position, vents were provided, and the metal was allowed to flow into the space where the wax had been. These casting processes, known since antiquity, were admirably adapted for industrial mass production of architectural ornament. In 1865, when he published his *Illustrations of Iron Architecture*, Daniel Badger with justice claimed that "whatever architectural forms can be carved or wrought in wood or stone, or other materials, can also be faithfully reproduced in iron" and that "the cost of highly-wrought and beautiful forms in stone and marble, executed with the chisel, is often fatal to their use; but they may be executed in Iron at a comparatively small outlay, and thus placed within the reach of those who desire to gratify their love of art, or cultivate the public taste."

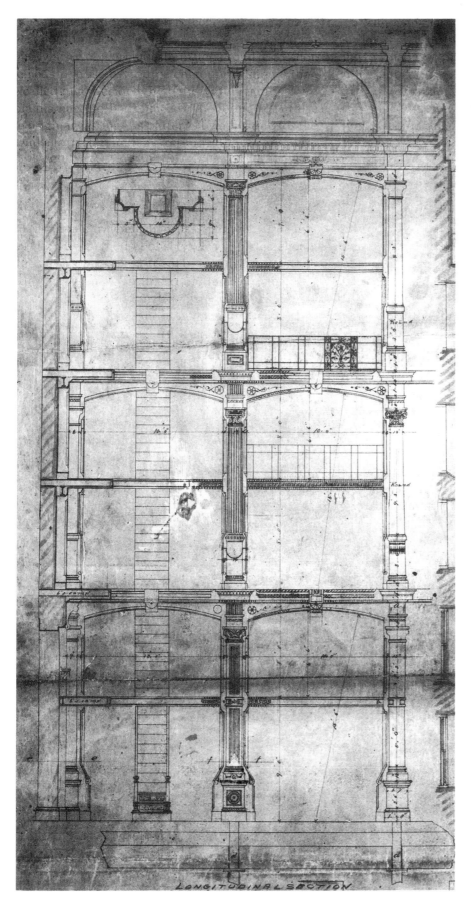

LONGITUDINAL SECTION

Peabody Institute architect Edmund G. Lind's May 1876 interior elevation of two full library bays shows some of its neo-Grec devices cast in iron by Bartlett, Robbins & Co. Illus.: The Archives of the Peabody Institute, Johns Hopkins University.

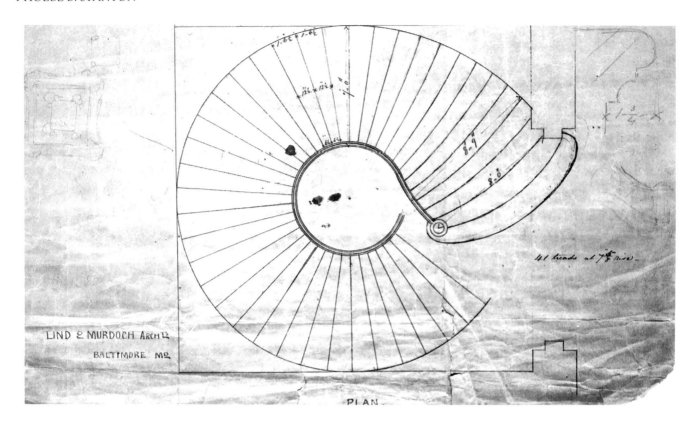

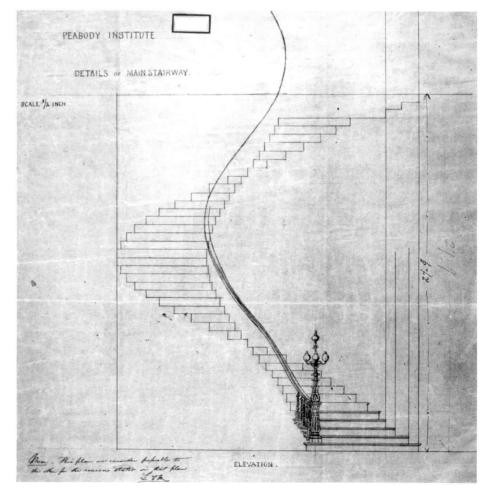

Lind's elevation for the magnificent cast-iron spiral staircase in the Peabody Institute building next door to the library illustrates a more elaborate newel post than the one that was installed and suggests some of the architect's and foundry's difficulties in executing the design. Illus.: The Archives of the Peabody Institute, Johns Hopkins University.

When, in 1857, George Peabody presented Baltimore with an endowment to create and support a cultural institution, and a building to house it became necessary, the trustees of the institute were forced to address questions raised by the relationships among function, cost, and style. The uses to which the building would be put were complex. There was a reasonable but limited sum to be spent on construction. Sensibly they decided to avail themselves of the qualities iron could offer. They also made up their minds on the question of style; they were from the outset convinced that although Gothic was a popular style they did not want to use it because it would not fit comfortably into Mount Vernon Place with its monument and splendid residences.

They resolved to open the design to competition, a questionable device, for architects had often been exploited by such an arrangement. The competition for the Peabody was no exception and complaints about its terms were promptly forthcoming in the national press. But the trustees soldiered on and selected what they defined as a "Grecian-Italian" design by a young architect, Edmund G. Lind, who had come from England in 1855 and was in practice in Baltimore. Lind produced a set of polished plans in 1858; James Crawford Neilson, a senior local architect, was designated to collaborate with him on practical details as the building developed. The trustees were convinced that the design they proposed would accord with "the quiet purpose of the building by its broad intervals, its distinct openings and its ample but classic proportions." As well as their respect for the architectural context of the new institute, they seem to have been inspired by the Renaissance Revival designs of Charles Barry and others for the new clubhouses on Pall Mall in London—buildings that must have been known to the trustees, who travelled abroad, often to England, where they could have been entertained in one or another of the clubs.

In their minutes, the trustees of the institute expressed their conviction that iron, readily available in Baltimore, was a practical expedient. The trustees, pragmatic gentlemen who insisted on control of costs, design, construction, and any flights of fancy the architect might experience, demanded durability and, later, when they undertook to build the new library, fireproof construction. But they were unwilling to carry iron prefabrication to its logical conclusion and accept buildings devoid of historical reminiscence and decorative detail.

The Peabody Institute building, the earlier of the two, was well underway when the Civil War overtook it and delayed its completion. It had been necessary to husband the building fund, for, when the institute was finally dedicated in 1866, the trustees were aware that, sooner rather than later, they would be forced to undertake construction of an additional structure to house the library. Because the Peabody's book collection was expanding prodigiously, it would quickly outgrow the room originally allotted it.

In the institute building iron was used sparingly, and it was employed in both structural and decorative ways. The complexity of the plan suggested employment of innovative building materials. The principal problem was the need for a two-story lecture hall (now the concert hall), above which there were to be, parallel with each other, two large rooms, oriented north-south and running the length of the hall below. The library would occupy the one on the east and, in that on the west, the Maryland Historical Society would have its headquarters. Because the interior space of the lecture hall was to be unobstructed, the floors of these rooms had somehow to be supported without bearing walls or piers below them.

Metal was the answer and, accordingly, four huge cast-iron trusses were set in the masonry outer walls of the building, east to west, at the height of the ceiling of the lecture hall. These were connected by girders to form a rigid framework on which the floor of the chambers above could rest. Perhaps because there was some feeling that this platform would not be adequate to carry the load of the library, which must have been immense, precautions for further support for the iron structural floor were provided. The wall between the two long rooms was built hollow and through its inner space cables under tension connected the iron girders to the wooden roof trusses. This construction resembled a bridge. In 1860–1861 Hayward, Bartlett & Co., Baltimore specialists in structural iron, supplied all these iron members at a cost of $15,000. The only iron visible in the lecture hall was in the slender columns beneath the balcony.

Externally the building was austere but elegant. Cubic in form, it was enriched only by the local marble of which it was constructed (the trustees had gone to great lengths to select a durable stone and one which would accord with the material of the Washington Monument) and by the decorative treatment of its windows, doors, quoins, and the iron railing on its west side. Interior decoration was confined to the

The newel post with an acorn finial and the graceful iron railing were furnished by Baltimore's Hayward, Bartlett & Co. in 1861 for $3,378.

plaster caryatids in the hall—cast in 1861 from a wooden original prepared by a local carver, James I. Randolph, who worked from an illustration, not of a Greek, but of a Roman example—plaster moldings, the marble floor of the lobby, and the splendid cantilevered cast-iron spiral staircase that rises the full height of the building at the east end of the lobby. In 1861 Hayward, Bartlett & Co., for $3,378, manufactured it from designs by Lind. Drawings in the archive of the institute reveal how he struggled to prepare a design that could be fitted into the available space. Its decoration can be defined as generally rococo in character, consisting of plants, flowers, and vines. It certainly was not Greek; that would come later.

By 1875 the library had grown to 60,000 volumes, so space was a problem and, because as many as a hundred readers visited it each day, so were heating and ventilation. The time had come for the anticipated addition of a new building to house it. Lind was again hired as architect to work, as he had earlier, in tandem with Neilson. In preparation for the great undertaking, Lind and Reverdy Johnson, a member of the board of trustees, went to New York to confer with James Renwick (1818–1895), a reigning arbiter of architectural taste who had designed the Smithsonian Museum. Later the trustees would call on Richard Morris Hunt (1827–1895), another fashionable architect, to render an opinion on how the front of the new building should be managed. The trustees and N. H. Morison, the provost, also studied the design of the Astor Library in New York, and there are in the minutes of the meetings of the building committee references to the two libraries with iron interiors in the old War and Navy departments Building in Washington (now the Executive Office Building). All of these were galleried chambers.

When he undertook the design of the library building Lind could have drawn on many sources for ideas. He had last practiced in England in the Midlands so he would have seen the Renaissance Revival that prevailed in Liverpool and other cities in the Midlands. He had, in fact, sailed for New York from Liverpool. As a student architect in London he had visited the Crystal Palace, and, when he travelled about, he had made a point of examining new and old buildings of note. He was a regular reader of *The Builder*, the leading English journal on architecture. He could have known firsthand, or seen illustrated, the Sailor's Home in Liverpool (1846–1848) by John Cunningham, which had a skylit interior court surrounded by five stories of iron galleries and a magnificent cast-iron entrance gate. *The Builder* had published an account and illustration of Peter Ellis's innovative Oriel Chambers (1864), also in Liverpool. There were books on construction, including William Fairbairn *On the Application of Cast and Wrought Iron to Building Purposes*, 1857–1858, in the Peabody Institute library. Iron was also being recommended for and widely used in American commercial architecture.

In addition, Lind was prepared for the challenge of the new building by the commission he had received in 1871 for the library at Hampden-Sydney College in Virginia where, within a rectangular brick outer shell, he had built a cast-iron interior of two floors surrounding an internal court with spiral staircases at the corners and an ornate gallery railing around the upper level of the stacks. This library was a prototype, a miniature version, of what he would build at the Peabody Institute. He had at hand the services of Bartlett, Robbins & Co. (the new name of what had been Hayward, Bartlett & Co.). It is not known whether this firm supplied the iron for the library at Hampden-Sydney, but it seems probable.

As they undertook construction of the Peabody Library, the provost and trustees were determined to acquire a fire-resistant structure, to unite the new with the earlier building in as seamless a way as could be accomplished, to make repairs to the interior and exterior of the latter (which had developed leaks in the roof because of its insufficient slope and poorly designed skylights), and to adapt to new uses the second-floor space that would be vacated by both the library and the Maryland Historical Society. Some of the space so acquired was to house the conservatory of music which had been operating off-site.

In 1878, as the new Library Building was being finished, the front of the institute was cleaned and its woodwork repainted; the balustrade at the roofline of the library had been continued along the north front and west side of the earlier building "to give greater elevation and greater beauty to the whole structure"; and "the steps at the hall entrance have been contracted to render them less conspicuous" and its interior and structure modified and renovated. The north front of the old and new buildings had been joined so expertly that they appeared as one.

Provost Morison celebrated what had been accomplished: "A more thoroughly built, substantial building could not easily be constructed. It is fire-proof throughout, and, where the new marble blocks interlock with the old not the slightest trace of settling can be found. Constructed from foundation to roof of brick, stone, iron, lime of Teil blocks, and copper, under as intelligent and faithful supervision as building ever had, I do not see why it may not rival the Pantheon itself in durability and permanence. I have watched its progress, with the keenest interest, from the laying of the first brick until now, visiting it two or three times every day, and as it rose, following it up to the highest ridge of its roof, and I have seen nothing but faithful, honest work, every where."[4]

The library stack room consists of masonry exterior walls surrounding and lending support to an iron interior frame, which, when the ground floor is included, is seven stories high. The internal rigid iron framework is composed of vertical supports, which are rectangular in section and run up from the foundations and out into the space at the top of the stack chamber, and wrought-iron beams that pass at each floor and each bay between the vertical members and the east and west walls. The mark of their manufacturer, the Phoenix Iron Company of Pennsylvania, was rolled into the beams. No attempt was made to hide the huge bolts that attach beam to column. The columns must consist of parts, as long as each floor is tall. The accuracy of their vertical alignment and the level of their tops would have been established as the framework was bolted together. This structural skeleton is hidden from view on the interior by decorative cast-iron dressings.

The cantilevered stair-case winds like a helix through the upper floors of the Peabody Institute building.

The room is surmounted by a series of masonry arches that form a cove, parts of which may be opened to permit the circulation of air. A grid of iron beams composes the visible portion of the roof; the glass of the interior skylight rests upon it. Above this skylight a huge chamber, beneath an outer roof with skylights, contains the iron roof trusses, supplied by the Kellogg Bridge Company of Buffalo. The Phoenix Iron Company fabricated the iron structure of the inner skylight. The forced-air ventilation system and the hot water heating apparatus were designed and supplied by Bartlett, Robbins & Co., which also manufactured the decorative iron skin that covers the frame on the interior. Warm air entered the chamber through cast-iron grills in the marble floor of the court and exited at the top of the room. The chamber was lighted by decorative gas fixtures.

In the course of their search for fire-resistant materials, the trustees interviewed a representative of the Fireproof Building Company of New York and concluded that the famous cement and artificial stone it marketed (manufactured at Teil, Ardeche, France, and which had won an award when exhibited at the Paris Exposition of 1867) were the best that could be found. The material of all the internal masonry in the library, including the arches at the top of the stack room, came from Teil. The choice of cast iron for the framework was wise; the blitz of the City of London would disclose that cast-iron frames stand up to fire even better than does steel. The floors of the stacks are composed of sheet iron panels that rest on the transverse beams. Further security against fire was provided by iron rolling shutters, produced by James Wilson of Baltimore. (It is unfortunate that many of these were removed in a recent renovation.) Wooden bookshelves were the only departure from fire-resistant materials.

In 1879 the trustees reported that, exclusive of the land but including fittings and furniture and the 1878 extensive renovation and improvement of the original institute building, they had invested $517,086 in the two structures. In a sense the library was the work of Bartlett, Robbins & Co.; receipts in the archive of the institute indicate that this firm received more than $100,000 for its part in construction.

Lind's skill in planning and design, his taste in decoration, and his ability to work with the members of the building committee (who were bossy) and the provost and the foundry were fundamental to the success of the venture.

This second building campaign, involving the construction of the library, also called for rearrangement of the spaces in the institute building to accommodate new uses when the library moved out. This was a planning challenge. The buildings were separated by a wide areaway, open on the south, and were to be connected only at the lobbies along the north front and via a brick-and-iron bridge at second-floor level across the south end of the areaway.

Reading from the ground up, the library building consisted of a sizable lecture hall, half in and half out of the earth, with windows at ground level (an arrangement that was possible because the site sloped to the east), a classroom parallel with the north front, satellite service rooms for lecturers, an office, staircases, and corridors. Lind shoehorned all this in around the iron supports of the internal frame as they rose from the footings. They appear in the plan and became part of the decorative treatment of the hall. This floor is now utterly changed to accommodate a small rehearsal room and two levels of bookstacks beneath part of the main floor.

The main floor, reached from the street by a tall flight of steps under a columned porch, is more than a half-story above street level. It contains a vestibule—

which appears to be a cube room, a bit of Lindian elegance—from which one could move into the lofty library reading room with huge windows that stretches to the east wall of the building. To its south is the stack chamber, sixty-one feet tall, containing six visible floors, the first being one foot taller than those above. There are windows on the outer sides of all but the sixth of the stack floors. The staff offices are beyond the stack room at the extreme south.

The next floor is more complex. Lind was asked to adapt to a new use the room in the institute building vacated by the library, and connect it with two rooms on the second floor of the new library building to create a U-shaped suite of three chambers. They would house the art collection, which, like the library, had been growing by leaps and bounds. Above the reading room of the library building he created a new room, as large as the one below, entered directly from the older building. This would be the sculpture gallery. It is one of the finest and best-proportioned spaces in the entire complex. Lind put art galleries in the room where the library had been and in the room on the south second floor of the library building contiguous with it. The reason for the bridge across the areaway becomes clear: it would connect the two buildings at this level in such

The stairway's rinceau pattern of running vines and leaves is a triumph of the founder's art.

a way that the library would be insulated from the rest of the institute. In the interests of fireproofing and separation of functions, the only direct connection above the main floor between the two structures was provided by the sculpture gallery, which did not, however, open into the library space and was separated from it by a heavy wall of fireproof blocks. There were iron doors wherever the two buildings approached one another. This discontinuity between the two parts of the institute required internal staircases—which were also iron—in the south ends of both buildings. The music conservatory was housed in the second and third floors along the west wall of the earlier building.

The ingenuity of Lind's plan is matched only by the glorious decoration of the stack room. The columns are covered with a veneer of decorative cast iron that is painted grey-green and touched with gold leaf. The ornament is Neo-Grec, a style that was often used in the nineteenth century in conjunction with Renaissance Revival architecture, and one which enjoyed considerable popularity in Baltimore buildings of the 1870s. It is called Neo-Grec because many of its details were taken from Greek decorative designs, well known from Owen Jones's *Grammar of Ornament* (1856), a copy of which was in the Peabody Library, and other pattern books. But in the nineteenth century such details were used at a scale and in ways that bear no relationship to their original appearance in Greek art, for most are extracted from the painted details on ancient pottery. The galleries are faced with a rich railing that used the Greek anthemion repeatedly. As is characteristic of the later nineteenth century, the decoration of this room is borrowed from historic ornament of various periods and these details are combined in an original way.

The Neo-Grec style is recognizable because of its Greek motifs, the symmetry of each part of the design, the use of plant forms with sharply pointed leaves, and the incised ornament which could be so effectively produced in iron casting. As in the decoration of the library, its motifs were often combined in ways (such as the pendants on the undersurface of the skylight, the delicacy of the plant forms in the incised ornament, their curvilinearity and pointed terminations) that suggest not Greek but the inspiration of Gothic—even of the illuminations in manuscripts—and Elizabethan decoration. Midway up the cast iron on the columns in the stack room of the library there is a small intaglio ornament that is axiomatic of this style. To all this, Lind added a splendid black and white marble floor in which are set cast-iron grates—formerly part of the

heating and ventilating system and now unfortunately covered.

Because the parts of the iron veneer were to be cast over and over again, Lind had only to draw one bay of the gallery railing, two column types and capitals—for that is all that are used in the library—and one of the decorative spandrel beams that bridge the bays at the level of the capitals on the second, fourth, and sixth floors, and to indicate where the various moldings for which he supplied patterns were to be applied. These details and the composition of the whole were his. Of course he had to get the designs right in the first place, decide exactly where he wished to put which of his patterns (not a mean responsibility), and see to it that the correct numbers of each molding and part were made for the job. When one stands in the center of the stack room and looks up, everything visible—from the floor through the crest of the moldings beneath the arches of the cove and the ceiling— is iron, attached with large screws and bolts. At ground level these screws were carefully countersunk, but high up under the masonry arches, no attempt was made to disguise the fastenings. There the cast iron is thin, and much of the actual decoration is sheet metal. The load-bearing iron structural frame is hidden beneath all this decoration.

Decoration is but a part of the design of the chamber. Its marvelous proportions are also owed to Lind. The six-story height is made more dramatic because there are but three columnar bays and each embraces two floors. Had there been a bay for each floor, the horizontal lines created by the capitals and the arches that join them would have made the ceiling appear lower than it is. The long dimension of the room is emphasized because the galleries and their railings on the ends are forward of the columns that are there engaged to the walls, a visual trick that pulls the walls back, qualifies the density of the ornament, and removes any possibility that the room might seem claustrophobic. In 1865 Badger had illustrated iron facades in which window openings on two floors are contained in one columnar bay. It can be said that Lind lined the interior of the library with a beautifully designed and custom-made cast-iron front.

It should be noted that the stack room was once even more handsome than it now is. The shelves that have been added in the middle of each bay tend to break the effects of height, airiness, and delicacy. But these additions were planned from the beginning to permit growth of the collection. Their weight was calculated into the load-bearing strength of the iron frame.

In the Peabody Institute and its library one can step back in time to appreciate Baltimore's past and sense the history of the city and the part it plays in life today. They give scale to the present and tell of the intellectual attainment, the building skills and the precision of the tastes of a century ago. The books in the library, the art collection of the institute, and the buildings belong together. They are a unique treasure and are inextricably a whole.

NOTES

1. The quotations from the German critic and the English commentator are both from an article "Influence of Construction on Style in Architecture," *The Foreign Quarterly Review*, April 1837. The German source is Hugo Ritgen and the title of his book (translated from the German) is *Contributions Relative to Constructions in Wood and Iron, and the Forming of a Character for a Newer and More Appropriate Species of Architecture*, Leipzig and Darmstadt, 1835.

2. The Baltimore *Sun*, April 24, 1849, reported that Benson's factory was in President Street and that he was producing decorative iron railings for cemeteries as well as demountable buildings. The shop of Lapouraille and Mauglin was at Falls Avenue and Pratt Street. Mr. Rhoads made houses with rubber roofs lined on either side with canvas. He was sending two sailmakers and two carpenters out with the houses "expenses paid and their clothes for 18 months. On arriving they will either work at their trades or dig gold, ½ their produce to go to the firm." The *Sun* on November 15, 1849, reported that K. McComas's shop was at Alice Anne Street and Harford Run [Central Avenue]. He had already made eighteen houses and had more in the course of construction.

3. The *Sun*, July 25, 1848, reported that Adam Denmead, who was an inventor as well as an iron founder, had three cupola furnaces in his plant and could melt eight tons of iron an hour. On December 27, 1848, the paper stated that, at his Monumental Iron Works, Denmead had built railway cars for the Washington branch of the Baltimore and Ohio Railroad. On January 3, 1849, it reported that the elegant rooms of the Temperance Temple in Gay Street, where only water was available at marble fountains, had a front and interior columns of cast iron "adorned with cornices of rich and classic finish" manufactured by Poole and Ferguson. On August 4, 1848, the *Sun* stated that Murray and Hazlehurst had an iron shop, called the Vulcan Works, at Federal Hill and were making the iron for a U.S. frigate under construction in the Gosport Naval Yards and all the machinery for the frigate *Susquehanna* then building in Philadelphia. In May 1849 they were reported to have built the iron boilers for the steamer *Powhatten* that was to run between Washington and Baltimore. The *Sun*, April 26, 1846, reported that James Millholland had built an iron bridge over Carroll's Run for the Baltimore and Ohio Railroad. It was made at Ellicott's rolling mill in Baltimore. On February 15, 1847, a new locomotive of his design, manufactured at the Bolton works, made the journey from Baltimore to Woodberry.

4. Peabody Institute Annual Report, 1878.

Wrought-iron gates, 1929, Maryland National Bank, Samuel Yellin, ironworker. Photo: Ron Haisfield.

V. ARCHITECTURAL IRONWORK

by
Robert L. Alexander

To complete the Washington Monument in Baltimore during the mid-1830s, architect Robert Mills (1771–1855) designed what is surely the outstanding example of decorative cast iron in the city. Between stretches of railings with diamond patterns, fascial posts support four sets of gates enriched by star-spangled panels. Pairs of tripods, designed after ancient Greek models, stand on the cheek blocks of each stairway by the entrances. The black surfaces of the ironwork, in strong contrast with the white marble of the great column and its base, mark the perimeter of the area commemorating the first president, the denser screening effect of the gates signalling the entrances. At the same time these decorative elements work with the cylindrical shaft and the cubical block to create an overall pyramidal composition.

Mills had planned a series of figural and decorative reliefs in bronze over the surface of the column. As these were eliminated because of expense, the iron fence and gates became the repository of references to the nation, the state, and Washington himself. The fasces referred to federal union, a prime concern of Washington's, protected by the strength symbolized by the axes and spearheads along the railings. The stars, signs of immortality to that age, also symbolized the thirteen original states—a circle of twelve in the gate panels plus a six-pointed one in the center that probably referred to the state of Maryland which erected the monument. Ancient Greeks used the tripod to burn offerings to deities, but for Mills and his contemporaries it was another symbol of immortality; he had employed the form on earlier monuments, and

here it commemorated the first president. Thus, while specific facts of the life of Washington are recorded in the bronze inscriptions composed by Mills and edited by John Quincy Adams, symbolism resides in the ironwork. Paving slabs outside the fence continued the patriotic motif by referring to the national colors; Mills could easily find the red and white, but for blue the architect had to substitute a gray stone.

Mills was involved in every aspect of the work. He wrote the contract for the fence and gates, which was signed on June 28, 1836. They were erected by May 24, 1838, at a cost of $5,000, and the tripods followed within a year. He made full-size drawings and visited the factory several times to supervise and correct the molds. The foundry, the Savage Manufacturing Company, was one of several operating around Baltimore, an area where iron had been worked since the eighteenth century.

The mold used for casting iron in such a foundry is usually of one piece, laid flat so that the iron flows into all areas. After it hardens, the face of the casting bears an imprint of any decorative detailing made on the mold. Molds of two or more pieces are used to make forms that are finished on both sides or that are

Robert L. Alexander, Professor Emeritus of Art History at the University of Iowa, is author of "Neoclassical Wrought Iron in Baltimore," Summer/Autumn 1983 Winterthur Portfolio, *and* The Architecture of Maximilian Godefroy; *and editor-in-chief,* The Papers of Robert Mills. *He has been studying and photographing Baltimore ironwork since the 1950s.*

The photographs accompanying this article, unless otherwise noted, are by the author.

Cast-iron railings and tripods, 1835–1839, Washington Monument, Robert Mills.

three-dimensional. The latter usually are cast hollow. Some parts, such as the railing of the monument, are relatively transparent, but cast-iron forms tend to widen out, employing surfaces and enriching ornament, as do the gate panels. The material often is opaque, calling attention to itself. The great advantage of this process is that many identical pieces can be reproduced from the mold, thus making it economical. A possible disadvantage is that the process invites elaboration in surface decoration.

Cast-iron gateway, 1838, Washington Monument, Robert Mills.

Quite a different material is wrought iron, which is produced by a forge and delivered to a blacksmith in the form of bars, straps, and rods. Unlike cast iron, it can be worked and reworked into a variety of shapes. In its tensile strength wrought iron differs from cast, so that it bends rather than breaking under great weight or pressure. It shapes are springy and muscular, and its decorative character grows out of the shapes themselves, rather than from surface ornament. The blacksmith produces an item for use in a specific place, whether a horseshoe or a stair railing, and each piece is likely to be unique, even when a pattern is followed.

Wrought- and cast-iron window guard, 807 Park Avenue, Andrew Merker, ironworker (?).

Wrought iron was customary for decorative work in the eighteenth and early nineteenth centuries; cast iron was known, but expensive. The two types might be used together, as in a window guard of a form popular in the 1850s and 1860s, for example at 807 Park Avenue, a few blocks west of the Washington Monument. Large horizontal and vertical bars establish the overall form, with straps of an eighth- to a quarter-inch to make up the C-scrolls that are the inner structure. Curvilinear patterns reflect the wiry, springy character of wrought iron, and transparency is its nature; the pattern is essentially one to be seen through. Cast-iron panels are heavy, inert, opaque, modelled on the surface for enrichment, and hang in suspension like medallions. In a pragmatic simplification of this pattern, straight bars are sometimes used to suspend the iron panels.

When Mills won the competition for the Washington Monument in 1814, he was building a national

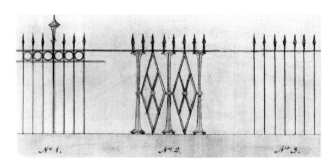

Drawings for three iron fences, 1837, Robert Mills. No. 2 is the fence used for the Washington Monument. Illus.: Hargrett Rare Book and Manuscript Library, University of Georgia.

reputation. He worked up and down the East Coast, but settled in Baltimore from 1815 to 1820 to supervise work on the monument. By 1830 he was established in Washington where he would produce such well-known works as the Treasury Building and that city's Washington Monument. He sent drawings for the Baltimore ironwork to the committee in charge and visited Baltimore as well as the Savage foundry. While thus engaged Mills was asked to supply designs for iron railings for the governor of Georgia. His drawing with three patterns survives, as does his covering letter of January 27, 1837, in which Mills estimated prices for the three different fences. Design No. 1, of wrought iron, cost $10 per running foot; design No. 2, of cast iron and identified further as "for the Washington Monument Baltimore," $6.40 per foot; and No. 3, the simpler wrought-iron design, $6.30 per foot. By the mid-1830s, then, the desire for a rich symbolic statement could be satisfied more economically with cast iron.

At this point two observations can be made. Although iron has often been used architecturally in nonstructural ways and is called decorative, in most cases the ironwork served a specific function. The list of uses is long: fences and gates, stair and area railings, stairways, guards for windows, doors, and other openings, the frames surrounding openings, balconies and trellises, roof crests, boot scrapers, brackets, clamps for tie-rods, fountains, hitching posts, signs, and lamps.

Further, most pieces of cast iron used decoratively were held within an armature of wrought iron; at the monument, wrought iron frames the gate panels and forms the top rail of the railings. On occasion this support has been reduced to a minimum. Three church fences designed by Robert Cary Long, Jr., during the 1840s, show a shift in preference by this young architect. His fence and massive gates for Benjamin Henry

Latrobe's Roman Catholic cathedral were designed and raised in 1841; the fence for his own church, St. Alphonsus (Park Avenue and Saratoga Street), in 1842; and for his Franklin Street Presbyterian Church (now the New Psalmist Baptist Church, Franklin and Cathedral streets), in 1847. In the first two he relied heavily on the frame of wrought iron, into which small elements of cast iron were attached to provide greater strength as well as ornament; they also received finials of cast iron. For the Franklin Street Presbyterian Church, wrought iron is restricted to the top and bottom rails and the rest is cast.

In the early nineteenth century the style of ironwork was neoclassical in keeping with the architectural taste. The French-born architect Maximilian Godefroy (1765–ca. 1842) reinforced this taste with the meander patterns and lachrymal vase terminals of his gates of 1814 for the cemetery at Westminster Presbyterian Church, Fayette and Greene streets. In the 1820 fence for his First Unitarian Church, a framework of verticals and horizontals is so adjusted that circles fill the small squares on two levels, and in the gates diagonal bars fill longer spaces. Where pieces come in contact, iron rivets or pins fasten them, so that the whole structure gains a great strength. Large square posts are set into the low granite wall at regular intervals, and braces add to the stability of the iron screen. The spearheads at the top show by the marks of the hammer that they also are of wrought iron, worked individually by the smith on his anvil. Small iron balls were introduced in the eighteenth century to maintain the clarity of a pattern by separating parallel lines. By the early nineteenth, they were being used in almost any joint where parts were pinned together, as here,

Wrought-iron gates, 1819–1820, First Unitarian Church, Charles and Franklin streets, Robert Walcott, blacksmith.

because they gave the smith some leeway in dimensions. It is not certain that Godefroy designed this fence, for the motif of circles was very common and has remained so to the present; Mills showed it in his design No. 1. This fence probably was designed by blacksmith Robert Walcott, who stamped his name at several places.

Signed pieces are rare, but there is another in Baltimore of almost the same date. At the south transept entrance of Latrobe's cathedral (Cathedral Street between Franklin and Mulberry streets, begun 1805) is a set of gates probably designed by William F. Small, who completed the cathedral sufficiently for use in 1821; the gates were added in the next year or two. They are stamped with the name of Martin Mettee, who was listed in city directories from 1818–1819 to 1855–1856. He was one of ten Mettees who practiced the craft over three generations. He also incised a series of Roman numerals on various parts. Because each part was handmade, they were not interchangeable and the numerals served as guides for assembling the gates in place.

From these pieces we see the neoclassical preference for simple geometric shapes—rectangles and circles, to which should be added the triangles and diamonds made by diagonal bars—and the meander pattern. Along with overlapping or tangent ovals, these shapes never lost their favor, as Mills's drawing and numerous later examples show; they account for a large part of surviving wrought iron. Often, however, they were overwhelmed by richer forms as tastes changed.

In Baltimore this enrichment began in the 1830s and 1840s, and a number of fine early-Victorian works survive. The stoop railing at 108 West Saratoga Street (1833–1834) has in the outer face three large panels,

Wrought-iron railing, 1834, 108 West Saratoga Street, Andrew Merker, ironworker (?).

two with lyres and in the center one a palmette, both motifs of the Greek Revival period. Most unusual is the manner in which these motifs have been formed. Each one is a single bar of iron bent into the shape, a job which only the master blacksmith would undertake because of the cost of the material. Additions have been pinned and welded to increase elaboration, add strength, and reduce the size of spaces left open. The borders too required much effort and skill. Semicircular straps of iron have been morticed where they cross each other, their ends dowelled and the middles pinned. The corner posts are most elaborate, with groups of four braces below and smaller scrolls above, all held together by collars, the universally employed fastener through the eighteenth century. It consists of a strip of iron bent hot around two or more pieces; as it cools, the iron exerts an increasingly tight grip around such elements as the group of scrolls and central post.

Wrought-iron railing, 1846, 106 West Saratoga Street, Andrew Merker, ironworker.

Next door, at 106 West Saratoga Street (1845–1846), the lyre appears again in the railings, and again flanked by concentric diamonds. Comparison with the railing of a decade earlier shows significant changes in technique. Instead of a single long bar forming the body of the lyre, two bowed C-scrolls on either side and another across the bottom are pinned together. The same small C-scrolls and broken scrolls are pinned on and strings are still attached by welding, but the base is drastically simplified. Thin strap is employed, and thus the risk of damaging the long bar of iron has been eliminated. The prominent diamonds lack the elegant curving sides. In the borders, morticing has been eliminated, and the circles, composed of thin strips of metal, have been strengthened by the C-scrolls pinned at top and bottom, their scrolled ends adding intricacy to the pattern. The intermediate diamond shapes, though formed separately, required no morticing. The manufacturing process has been altered by the introduction of a number of small forms that could be made with some assurance by apprentices, without great financial risk. Complex operations requiring much skill and experience have been reduced and eliminated. Numerous examples of this form of lyre occur throughout the city, from Broadway in Fells Point to Washington Boulevard in the west.

Evidently the blacksmith's shop had become the scene of mass production, with a primitive form of assembly line making use of the varied skills of the workers. Many reasons can be offered to explain this change—financial pressures and perhaps inflation, the use of less substantial materials made available by modern industry, an expanding population with a taste for effect yet satisfied with less skillful work and possibly lower quality—but the 1840s did witness an increasing use of cast iron. Perhaps in this early stage there was a fear of competition from the cheaper material, although the two were often used together by the same artisan. Here, for example, the posts are cast iron.

The blacksmith of the last railings is known, in this case because his bill to the client has been preserved. He was Andrew Merker, an emigrant from Germany to Baltimore in 1831 who was responsible for much of the decorative iron of these decades. Merker probably made the type of window guard seen at 807 Park Avenue, for his son William drew it in a notebook about 1850. It is significant that the client went to a blacksmith rather than an architect for the design of the ironwork, a circumstance that proliferated with mass-produced cast iron.

The taste for richness and intricacy of detail continued in the wrought iron of the latter part of the century. At 107 West Saratoga Street (the central house of three built just after the Clay Street fire of 1873), stair railings were installed. The diagonal railings are composed of tubular iron worked into a series of scrolls. This form had developed in the 1840s and was moderately popular for about fifteen years, but it did not become a new fashion. The narrow spaces of the stoop railings are filled with small parts to achieve intricacy; large and small C-scrolls with elements looking like vine tendrils are held to the upright by a collar. The pin and ball, formerly so common, had disappeared with this

Wrought-iron railing, circa 1874, 107 West Saratoga Street.

revival of the older device. Another idea drawn from the European past, the German Baroque, is the iron vegetation rising from the top rail. The railing beside the basement steps has a large circle quartered by incurved strips of metal. This motif derives from the late eighteenth and early nineteenth centuries and is thus a sign of the Colonial Revival then getting underway. This small group of railings represents several of the trends of the period.

The neo-Baroque element appears also in the balconies of Belvidere Terrace (1876–1880). The ironwork consists largely of heavy strap iron bent to form the bulging curves, with short wavy straps, and heavier bars carrying ball and vase-shaped terminals. Sheet metal plaques fit into the bulge, with holes cut into their lower surfaces and spiralling scrolls welded to the upper faces. Obvious rivets emphasize the joints of the structure. The vigor and burly strength of this ironwork seems an expression of the developing industrial age. Enhancing the link with the neo-Baroque

Wrought-iron balcony, circa 1880, Belvidere Terrace, 1000 block North Calvert Street, J. B. Noel Wyatt, architect.

intricacy of the railings at 107 West Saratoga Street, the iron flowers of the latter reappear above the gables of the first house of Belvidere Terrace, 1000 North Calvert Street. This house had been built by Benjamin C. Howard in 1830, and its massive renovation became the first step in a new Howard land development. The architect for this terrace in the Queen Anne style was J. B. Noel Wyatt, and he undoubtedly designed the ironwork as well.

By the midnineteenth century, industrialization had made cast iron cheap and common. (Cast iron could be produced for three cents a pound in 1851.) Yet for a long time cast iron emulated the patterns and appearance of wrought, for example, in the heavy grills in the windows of the Provident Savings Bank (1903), Howard and Saratoga streets.

Imitation is prominent in a mass-produced cast-iron design used widely in the 1850s and 1860s. Making up a fence at 112 West Mulberry Street, the panel comprises two large C-scrolls enclosing a central oval, small C-scrolls enclosing palmettes at top and bottom, and two fleurs-de-lys held by small S-scrolls. Even the ball and pin connection is imitated. Each motif is drawn from the vocabulary of wrought iron, but the rounded surfaces and edges are those of cast iron. In addition, numerous contacts between forms are nec-

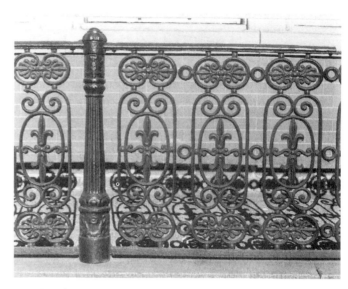

Cast-iron fence, circa 1851, 112 West Mulberry Street.

essary so that the molten metal can flow throughout the mold and increase the overall strength. The form is cast as a panel, and a series is held within top and bottom horizontals of wrought iron. Supports for the fence are rather heavy posts cast in three dimensions as a column with floral ornament at top and bottom. This house was built in 1835–1836, but the fence, like the top story, was undoubtedly a later addition.

Cast-iron balcony, circa 1854, 700 Cathedral Street, Niernsee and Neilson, architects.

Detail, cast-iron balcony, 700 Cathedral Street. Photo: Ron Haisfield.

The posts, however, can be dated by their use in a stoop at 6 East Franklin Street (1850–1851), where they appear with railings of wrought iron. The panels appear again in a wrought-iron armature for the side balcony (about 1854) at 700 Cathedral Street. Employed generously, they form pilasters, railing, and upper screen. These panels may have been cast in Baltimore, since they were used so profligately, but the same panels have been used for fences and railings in Washington, D.C., and Charleston, South Carolina, perhaps imported from Baltimore.

In another early cast-iron panel the forms of wrought iron have a rigidity. With a central wheel-like medallion, C-scrolls, and palmettes, the panels appear as window guards at 208 West Monument Street and 14 East Mt. Vernon Place. Another version was used at the recently renovated Hackerman House (1847–1848), 1 West Mt. Vernon Place, transformed into square panels, with diamonds, floral motifs, and other fillers. Both the narrow and the square panels were mass-produced as interchangeable parts, for the latter appear again around the corner at 601-607 Washington Place. The unusual wheel design may have originated in either form, but the motifs drawn from wrought

iron have been used for their decorative value and lack their original linear vibrancy. A constraint arises from the need to have all parts in close contact, so that scroll ends do not spring out into space. The need for continuous channels in the molds to allow the free flow of the molten iron also limited the freedom of the design.

In addition, the two structures on Mt. Vernon Place share another use of cast iron: the window lintels with modillioned cornices and elaborate palmettes. That at 1 West is fuller, protrudes from the wall farther, has smaller modillions, and is carried by two iron brackets. The parts may have been cast separately, so that the palmettes could be combined with different cornices.

Baltimore has many examples of the cornice with a central palmette, and clearly several different molds were used for the floral element. A variation on the one already seen appears at 21-21½ East Centre Street and 707-709 St. Paul Street. Another type without the scroll

Window guard and cornice of cast iron, 1848, Hackerman House, 1 West Mt. Vernon Place.

base for the palmette was also popular, with one mold represented at 22 West Monument Street and 219 West Madison Street. Very similar, but from a different mold, are the lintels at 824 Park Avenue and 704 North Howard Street, and a variant is on the Enoch Pratt House at 201 West Monument Street. (The Pratt House, now part of the Maryland Historical Society, also has fine roof cresting, another common use of cast-iron decoration.) The lintels at 113 West Saratoga Street have an awkward but strong palmette with large scrolls like headlights. In an extraordinary variant, at 10 West Madison Street, cornucopias and foliage replace the palmette. But this example is more interesting because it is wood carved in imitation of cast iron, and its bulkier (rather than more delicate) forms and broad surfaces (instead of wiry lines) testify to a change in taste brought about by the industrial product.

These lintels and palmettes were undoubtedly designed and cast by different manufacturers and could be selected by the architect, builder, or client. Catalogs, such as that of Bartlett, Robbins & Co., showed an increasing number of cast-iron architectural parts, and they survive in many buildings of the present.

Best use of the economies of mass production required the casting of identical panels to be fastened together to fill the space available. Through the later nineteenth century this practice continued, as designers sought new sources of inspiration. The panels of the window guard at 336 St. Paul Street might have come directly from an eighteenth-century pattern book, but the cast iron produces grosser forms than the linear wrought iron. For the balcony at 14 West Madison

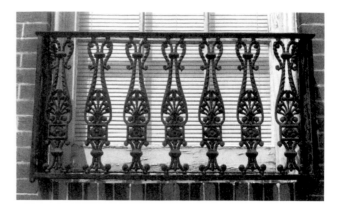

Cast-iron window guard, 336 St. Paul Street.

Street, the designer chose the interlace that was popular in the Germanic world from the fifteenth century onward, but he substituted a flat pattern for the interweaving of rods of metal.

Another way of achieving continuity across the whole surface arises from the necessary linkage of the parts. Repetition of identical forms occurs in the balcony at 28 East Mt. Vernon Place (1853), but with a difference. Instead of a series of whole, individual panels, each large arch shares a supporting column on either side; at one end the outer column is missing. Although not a sophisticated manner of filling the space, it has the advantage of being adaptable to spaces of differing lengths.

The popular grapevine pattern readily gives the illusion of continuity as the vine seems to grow upward and outward. A very skillfully designed example appears in the balconies on Broadway at Baltimore

Cast-iron balcony, 14 West Madison Street.

Cast-iron balcony, 28 East Mt. Vernon Place.

Detail of grapevine pattern, balcony, Broadway and Baltimore Street. Photo: Ron Haisfield.

Street, from the latter part of the century. The sense of separate panels almost disappears. For all its transparency, each protruding part broadens as it recedes, echoing the shape of the mold, and here even the collar of wrought iron is imitated in cast.

Waverly Terrace (1850–1851) on Franklin Square, designed by the architect Thomas Dixon, had elegant

balconies and fences of cast iron. The still-extant balconies achieve continuity through large panels of curvilinear patterns derived from seventeenth- and eighteenth-century wrought iron. They even have the transparency of the latter, in contrast with the density of the fences that once stood at ground level.

Cast-iron balconies, Broadway and Baltimore Street. Photo: Ron Haisfield.

Stamped metal cornice, circa 1874, 107-109 West Saratoga Street.

This same supervision was possible in a different type of material that appeared after the middle of the century—sheet metal architectural ornament. Of galvanized iron or terne (sheet iron coated with an alloy of lead and tin), the thin metal could be stamped out in dies, cut, bent, and soldered into a variety of shapes. For the most part this work was confined to cornices on building fronts and lintels for doors and windows. Such a cornice runs across the buildings at 107-109 West Saratoga Street, the site of the wrought-iron railings discussed earlier. In the same year John G. Hetzell's advertisement in Howard's *The Monumental City* illustrated a cornice almost identical with the one on these houses. (For a simpler form, see Waverly Terrace.) It emulates wood in its right-angle junctions of parts and in the appearance of drilling, jigsawing,

Cast-iron balconies and fences, 1850–1851, Waverly Terrace, 100 block North Carey Street, Thomas Dixon, architect. Photo: circa 1936, HABS, Library of Congress.

Dixon was able to retain control over his work because the cast-iron parts were not yet available as catalog items. During the early part of the century, such major architects as Latrobe and Mills, Charles Bulfinch, John Haviland, and William Strickland employed cast iron as well as wrought. Not only through the drawings, but by supervision of work at the factory, Mills exercised control over the finish and quality of the work. This control was feasible during the pre-industrial period when factories were small, runs were limited in number, and work was customarily made to order. We know from their writings that men like Latrobe and Mills were much concerned with the faithful execution of their designs. The system made their close supervision possible before midcentury, when large runs began to prevail.

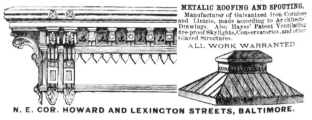

Advertisements for Gustav Krug, successor to Andrew Merker, and John G. Hetzell, in George W. Howard's The Monumental City, *1873, p. 408.*

Detail, gate, Maryland National Bank. Photo: Ron Haisfield.

plant elements is a measure of his skill. Instead of relying on rivets and pins, he revived the collar for the back-to-back C-scrolls and the plants. Benchwork—cutting and hammering cold sheet metal into the foliate and floral shapes which are then welded onto the scrolled stems—was another long-used technique. While conforming to the emphasis on outline, the plants present an Art Deco stylization. Repetition of a few motifs characterizes wrought-iron compositions, providing here a dazzling exhibition of the decorative intricacy of great ironwork.

Although Baltimore has lost much of its wrought ironwork, a great deal survives and, indeed, is still being produced. Andrew Merker, who made so much of it in the midnineteenth century, hired Gustav Krug in 1848. The latter founded the firm now known as G. Krug and Son, Inc., which still creates decorative iron for the city and a large region around Baltimore.

Samuel Yellin, of Philadelphia, one of the great artisans in wrought iron, forged this horse's head newel post for the Maryland National Bank, Baltimore and Light streets, in 1929. Photo: Ron Haisfield.

and carving, all aspects of the newly popular Eastlake style which was based on the appropriate use of wood. Produced in small shops, this material became a sensitive measure of taste in its changing form over the decades, for, as Hetzell stated in his ad, the pieces were "made according to Architects' Drawings."

All of these kinds of ornament have continued into the twentieth century. In the case of wrought iron, however, the material has changed, for now a type of steel is employed. A prime example is the series of entrance gates and the array of grilles along the central banking hall of the Maryland National Bank Building, Baltimore and Light streets (1929), which form one of the outstanding displays of the artistry of Samuel Yellin (1885–1940) and his large shop in Philadelphia. Reviving techniques of the Medieval, Renaissance, and Baroque periods, Yellin became the outstanding craftsman in the medium. Consistency in the twisted verticals, the curving C-scrolls, and the undulating

Part Two

DIRECTORY OF BUILDINGS

T he ten buildings with full iron facades, plus sixteen others with iron storefronts, described on the following pages, represent virtually all that is left of Baltimore's cast-iron architecture. This category once included hundreds of such specimens, which held special meaning for the city. Among those that remain there are a few surprises and several diamonds in the rough, for so far just one has been completely renovated.

1. 300 WEST PRATT STREET, 1871
BARTLETT, ROBBINS & CO., FOUNDRY (?)

This signal preservation success makes an especially stately appearance at night when quartz halogen lamps light its glowing facade. It is Baltimore's most intact, visible, and accessible cast-iron front. In a prime location, with two new wings, 300 West Pratt Street is embarking on a second career as an office building, altogether a dramatic turnaround for the formerly dingy and abandoned industrial structure.

Its story began in 1843 when William Wilkens, a German immigrant, came to Baltimore and began making brushes from hog bristles, and stuffing for upholstered furniture from horse and cattle hair. His business expanded and in 1847 he relocated to Frederick Road near the slaughterhouses that supplied his raw material. By the early 1870s, Wilkens's 165 acres of grounds included a factory, brickyard, blacksmith shop, and tenant houses for his 700 employees, who turned out twenty tons of steamed "curled hair" a week. Some of it was woven into haircloth, an incredibly durable covering for stuffed furniture; some was made into women's hairpieces and wigs. Wilkens had a national market for his products, and offices in New York.

For his local headquarters, he erected an office and warehouse building at 300½ West Pratt Street, connecting it to his Frederick Road factory with Baltimore's first telephone. The new facility was in the center of the business district, close by the harbor's ships and piers. The Baltimore and Ohio Railroad ran in front of the property and it is possible that the cast-iron front for Wilkens's new building arrived by rail, probably from the Bartlett, Robbins & Co.'s foundry, located at Pratt and Scott streets, just east of the B&O's Mt. Clare depot.

The column capitals and the large consoles at the roofline closely resemble those on Plate 12 of the Bartlett, Robbins & Co. catalog, and on the Richmond iron fronts produced by the same organization (pages viii, ix, x, 87). The Renaissance Revival style is less severe than it may seem at first. Consider the intricate molding over the arches on the upper levels, the projecting units terminating the intermediate cornices, and the quoins running up and down the sides with alternate paneled and vermiculated units representing dressed and undressed masonry. A line of rope molding stretches across the building above the top floor.

The stories typically diminish in height as they ascend. One reason for such foreshortening was to give the upper floors an illusion of greater height according to the rules of perspective, but there was a practical aspect as well, for the top floors were used mainly for storage and therefore didn't need as much light. Also,

Flanked by the Bromo-Seltzer Tower and a new addition, the restored cast-iron facade of 300 West Pratt Street stands out with a luminous glow at dusk.

Hayward, Bartlett & Co., Baltimore's nationally known architectural foundry, cast the intricate column capitals and scrollwork for the iron storefront at 202-206 West Pratt Street.

the higher they were, the more human or mechanical effort was needed to reach them. In a nineteenth-century warehouse building, the lower floors, where merchants displayed their goods and took orders, demanded the greatest amount of light, especially the storefront, whose broad expanse of plate glass lit the merchandise and provided a view from the street. Window-shopping began with cast-iron architecture.

This building is actually a double warehouse, a common type in nineteenth-century Baltimore, divided front to back, top to bottom, usually by a masonry bearing wall. The wall was mainly for support because the fifty-foot width of this building—others were wider—was too great to span practically with timber floor joists. Wrought iron was too expensive to use, and steel was unavailable for commercial construction. The wall, seen outside as a pilaster in the middle of the storefront, might also separate tenants occupying different halves of the building.

The iron front was literally a facade normally applied to a conventionally constructed wood and masonry building behind it, and attached to it by various means. At 300 West Pratt Street, the three brick bearing walls, each twenty-two inches thick, fill the voids in back of the iron pilasters at the sides and center. Bolts and screws hold the metal to the brick, and wrought-iron tie-rods nailed to the floor joists further lock the iron front to the rest of the structure. The interior timber construction is heavy, befitting a warehouse.

By 1910, Wilkens had shifted his headquarters back to the Frederick Road factory, and thereafter rented the Pratt Street building to a succession of paper firms. The last was the Robins Paper Company, which bought the structure in 1939 and occupied it until 1972 when the city acquired it. The Wilkens-Robins Building then stood vacant and was in danger of demolition. However, following a strong effort to save it, the city in 1988 awarded the building to Stone and Associates, which had presented a redevelopment plan incorporating office space, a restaurant, and the Baltimore Visitors Center.

The architect, RTKL, Inc.; the contractor, Lawrence Construction Company; and the cast-iron restoration specialist, Steven T. Baird, Architect and Associates, faced a major challenge. The column capitals and other details had been stripped off the building in the 1940s. Owners often did this when wrought-iron fastenings rusted and heavy pieces of iron decoration began plummeting to the sidewalk. The outside walls were four inches out of plumb due to the demolition of structures on either side, and the fire department had tested its new saws inside by cutting automobile-sized chunks out of the floors.

In the course of restoration, the missing metal details were recast in aluminum and refastened, and heavy structural steel was added inside to provide lateral bracing for the walls and longitudinal support for the floor joists. A new five-story curtain wall building with a prefinished aluminum sunscreen was added to the sides and back of the old structure and connected to it inside, adding 36,000 square feet of floor space to the original 25,400. Both sides of the addition are set back from the cast-iron facade, in effect framing it. This was due less to a design decision than to the city's master plan to reconfigure Pratt Street as a boulevard, which required setbacks of fifty feet for new structures. The $10 million project has been renamed the Marsh & McLennan Building after its major tenant, an insurance firm, and officially renumbered 300 West Pratt Street. It won the 1990 grand award from the Baltimore chapter of the American Institute of Architects.

Circa 1953 photo: The Peale Museum, Baltimore City Life Museums.

LLOYD'S BALTIMORE ELEVATED BUILDING MAP

The 300 and 400 blocks of West Baltimore Street, shown here, compose the city's cast-iron district. They contain six of Baltimore's ten buildings with complete metal facades (numbered 2-7), and three of its iron storefronts (two of them appear on the map, 14 and 16). Spared by the 1904 Baltimore fire and beyond the reach of recent redevelopment projects, the blocks exist today, physically anyway, much as they did a hundred years ago; the north side of the 400 block is virtually unchanged. But the merchants and the garment workers who toiled here have mostly gone, and the bustling commerce and street life that once enlivened the district have departed with them.

Baltimore Street was historically the city's major business thoroughfare. A century ago, five- and six-story buildings had replaced most of the three-story ones dating from the town's earliest days. Awnings extended out to the curb, and walking beneath them, amidst the variety of colorful wares displayed on the sidewalk, must have been an exhilarating experience. In the streets, horsecars vied with horse-drawn carriages and drays, and with workmen maneuvering two-wheeled pushcarts or wheelbarrows. The traffic jams and the deafening noise of the iron tires on the cobblestones must have been as bad as, or worse than, the present high-speed rumble of automobiles and trucks through the city.

On the loft floors above street level, employees struggled with newly introduced devices that would define the twentieth-century office building—elevators, typewriters, and telephones—while scores of men, women, and children, many of them Jewish immigrants from Eastern Europe, along with some Irish and Italians, labored to assemble everything from cigars and stoves to shoes, overcoats, and umbrellas. The same front office intrigues and backstairs assignations that take place today probably went on then. In the evening after the workers went home, private carriages rattled through the shadowy, gaslit streets, bearing their well-dressed occupants to the city's lively restaurants and theaters.

Presently, several businesses remain in the area, and some owners of iron-front buildings are aware of their commercial potential. Artists—the shock troops of urban redevelopment—have begun to filter into the neighborhood. Its future would be less uncertain if the cast-iron fronts on these two blocks could receive the same treatment as 300 West Pratt Street.

MAP KEY
2. 307-309 West Baltimore Street
3. 322 West Baltimore Street
4. 407 West Baltimore Street
5. 409 West Baltimore Street
6. 412 West Baltimore Street
7. 414 West Baltimore Street
14. Abell Building, 329-335 West Baltimore Street
16. 419 West Baltimore Street

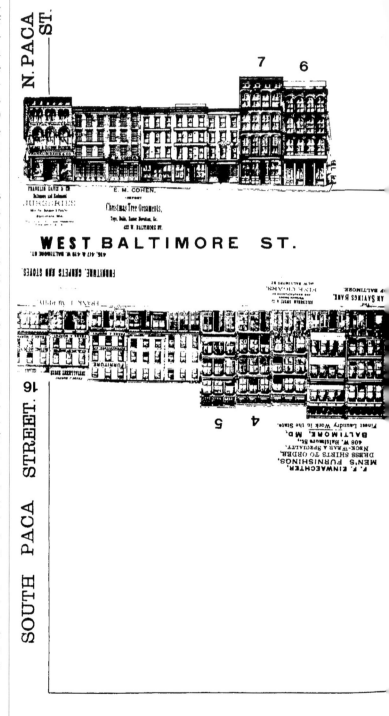

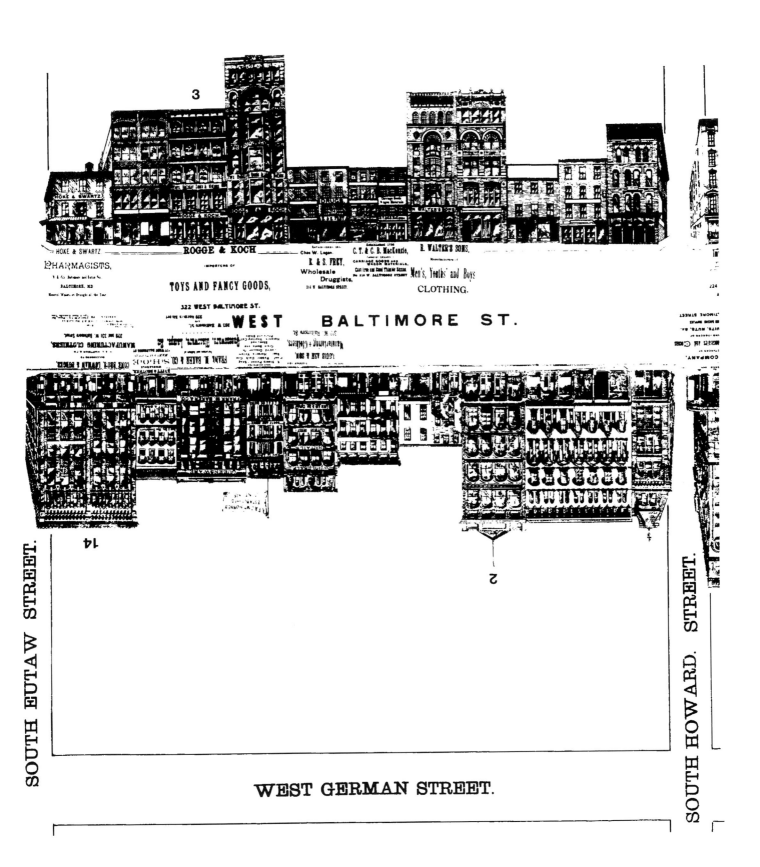

"*Lloyd's Baltimore Elevated Building Map of the Five Hundred Million Business District of Baltimore*," 1891. *Projected by J. T. Lloyd, photographed by Isaac Friedenwald. From an original in the Geography and Map Division, Library of Congress.*

wholesale boot and shoe business on the upper three floors and leased the rest to clothing firms. In 1889, Pearre Brothers and Company, wholesale dry goods and notions, moved in. About this time, the building's roofline acquired a parapet and a flagpole, but these elements were gone again by 1910. William Keyser, a Baltimore entrepreneur active in coal, iron, copper, stockyards, and railroads, acquired the building in 1895. (After the Baltimore fire of 1904, Keyser was appointed to head the Burnt District Commission that supervised the rebuilding of the city's mercantile center.) Frank and Adler and other wholesale boot and shoe firms occupied it in the first two decades of this century, followed by more companies dealing in men's furnishings.

About 1940, the property changed hands again. The new owners installed black Carrara glass panels above the original storefront and opened a retail men's clothing store, the Trading Post. Later alterations produced the present storefront with display windows flanking a recessed entrance. A single cast-iron column was left in the center, covered with stainless steel.

However, the rear of the building, facing Redwood Street, which is six stories high due to the slope of the site, offers more cast iron on the street-level loading

2. 307-309 WEST BALTIMORE STREET, CIRCA 1875
BENJAMIN F. BENNETT, BUILDER.
BARTLETT, ROBBINS & CO., FOUNDRY (?)

Benjamin F. Bennett was a prominent and prolific Baltimore contractor who built the Broadway Market, Mt. Vernon Place Methodist Church, "and numerous private residences of more or less pretension to beauty and ornamentation," according to a trade book of the time. Bennett used a vignette of this building in his advertisement in George W. Howard's *The Monumental City,* ca. 1876, (p. 452).

Its currently neglected iron facade so closely resembles the restored 300 West Pratt Street, two blocks south, that they may have been cast by the same foundry, Bartlett, Robbins & Co. The similarities include the storefronts, and the upper-level columns, arches, spandrels, quoins, and rope molding. However, there are also subtle differences. The Corinthian capitals and the distinctive paired consoles supporting the main cornice are almost exactly the same as those on the Richmond blocks (page x), fabricated by Baltimore's Hayward, Bartlett & Co.

Bennett constructed 307-309 West Baltimore Street for Harford County's Faust Brothers, who operated a

BENJ'N F. BENNETT,

NORTH CHARLES STREET.

CONTRACTOR AND BUILDER,

No. 44

S. HOWARD STREET,

BALTIMORE.

SECOND STREET.

BALTIMORE STREET.

dock and the floor above; it varies somewhat from the Baltimore Street elevation.

3. 322 WEST BALTIMORE STREET, CIRCA 1867
GEORGE H. JOHNSON, ARCHITECT.
BARTLETT, ROBBINS & CO., FOUNDRY.

Even in disarray this building retains its architectural integrity. It is the most ornate cast-iron front in the city and one of the most venerable. The extreme alterations at street level compose a study in themselves.

The provenance of the design can be traced from New York through Richmond to Baltimore in the person of George H. Johnson. From its similarity to a storefront depicted in New York founder Daniel D. Badger's well-known catalog, *Illustrations of Iron Architecture*, 1865 (Plate XV, No. 7), and to contemporaneous iron-front buildings in Richmond designed by Johnson and produced by the Baltimore foundry, Hayward, Bartlett & Co. (pages viii, ix, x), the conclusion is all but inescapable that Johnson was the architect of 322 West Baltimore Street and that Bartlett, Robbins & Co. (the successor firm) supplied the ironwork.

George H. Johnson, an Englishman, arrived in the United States in 1851 and became Badger's foremost architect. He devised a great number of cast-iron modules for his employer and when he established his own firm, Johnson recombined these basic patterns in various ways for his clients. The collaboration with the Hayward-Bartlett-Robbins organization on the iron fronts in Richmond, and subsequently on the one in Baltimore, is a good example of this procedure, for elements of all three Richmond buildings show up on 322 West Baltimore Street: the solid balustrades from the Sterns Block, the cornice from the Branch Building, and the facade and window treatment from the Donnan Block. (In 1871, Johnson was in Chicago promoting his own invention for fireproofing buildings: the use of hollow terra cotta tile for constructing subfloors and partitions; his ideas had an important impact on later commercial architecture.)

We further know, from an illustration in the border of the 1869 Sachse "Bird's-Eye View of Baltimore," that each window opening on the upper floors of 322 West Baltimore Street originally held two round-headed windows, side by side, and that the ground floor was similarly arranged (with double doors substituted for the windows). The storefront in this configuration also appears in the 1891 "Lloyd's Baltimore Elevated Building Map." Between that time and 1895,

however, when the structure was shown again in a Baltimore trade publication, the street-level arches were removed, most of the doors were replaced by window sashes, and terra cotta tiles in Classical Revival forms were placed over much of the cast iron. In the twentiethth century the ground floor was renovated a second time, probably when it was divided for two tenants. Some of the original material doubtless exists underneath but what one sees is a singular instance of clay imitating metal imitating stone.

The upper four floors of cast iron, reduced in height at the top, are essentially unchanged, and are unique in Baltimore. A front rank of fluted columns set on pedestals runs floor-to-floor. Within them is another set of columns, whose twisted shafts support arches with Corinthian keystones. Pilasters adorn the sides of the building, ending in large consoles decorated with lion's heads. This rich assembly of components, and the deeply modeled facade, make a striking impression on the street.

Alberti, Brink and Company, importers of fancy goods and notions, were the first occupants. In the late 1870s, they were replaced by Rogge and Koch, basically in the same business, plus toys. In the 1880s, this firm had thirty-five workers on the premises, six salesmen on the road, and was described as the largest operation of its kind in the United States. By then, they had added "an A1 line of musical instruments, pipes, [and] druggists' sundries," and expanded into leased space in the adjacent, taller building to the east, whose projecting central bay is covered with sheet metal—galvanized iron or zinc—a late-nineteenth-century development. In 1895, the company had fifty employees and nationwide sales, but one partner, Christian Rogge, died that year and the restructured William Koch Importing Company departed the building in 1903.

There followed in the twentieth century a succession of garment industry and other firms. At one time or another between 1930 and 1940, 322 West Baltimore Street housed the College Cut Clothing Company, the LeMay Cloak and Suit Company, Stanley Men's Shop, the Exclusive Tailors, as well as Aarco Oil and Gas, Union Distillers Products Company, and Baltimore Table Tennis Courts (on the second floor). Vacancies appeared in later decades, but as this is written, artists appear to have taken up residence on the upper loft floors.

4. 407 WEST BALTIMORE STREET, CIRCA 1875

Although presently paired with its iron-front neighbor to the west, the building shown on the left in the photograph—407 West Baltimore Street—once had a real twin to the east. It appears as "Buckingham, Swope and Company, Fine Cigars," on "Lloyd's Baltimore Elevated Building Map."

Above the brick storefront and boxed-in cornice at 407 West Baltimore Street is a plain but practical metal front of a type that was once common in Baltimore: chamfered iron piers with floral capitals, scrolled consoles, and a paneled frieze and cornice, here painted in shades of cream and brown.

Built as an investment property for Samuel Stein and Brothers, clothing manufacturers and bankers, this used to be known as the L. Frank and Sons building, for the shoe manufacturer who occupied it from 1878 to 1886. The first tenant was Charles Weatherby, dealer in iron ranges and furnaces. In 1890, the Dannenberg Manufacturing Company's fifty operatives produced infants' wear on the upper three floors. A. J. Strauss and Company, pants manufacturers, owned the building in 1898, and in 1919, Osias Schonfeld bought it and ran the New York Fancy Cake Bakery on the first floor until it was replaced by the Traffic Cafeteria.

However, the upper stories continued to house tailors and other garment-related industries until quite recently. The present owner acquired the building in 1973 and a decade later joined it to the structure next door with the continuous street-level brick facade. It is now a discount apparel store.

5. 409 WEST BALTIMORE STREET, CIRCA 1875

The Rieman Brothers erected the structure on the right in the photograph, and the Hess Brothers were their first tenants. Initially, Henry Rieman operated a wholesale grocery business on this site. When he died he left the three-story brick house on the property to his sons: Alexander, a railroad president; William J., a commission merchant; and Joseph, a developer. (One of Joseph's projects was the Rieman Block, an imposing Victorian commercial and residential complex on West Lexington Street.)

The Rieman Brothers replaced their father's property with a "four story iron warehouse." Above the modern brick storefront, which was added in the past decade, it is virtually unchanged.

The Riemans' first tenant, 1876–1883, was the N. Hess and Brother boot and shoe factory. Nathan Hess, shoemaker, emigrated from Germany in 1852 and began making shoes twenty years later in Baltimore with his brother Sol. When Nathan died, his son Isaac took over the business, opening a retail store on Baltimore Street supplied by the factory. Later on, Isaac brought his sons into the firm. It became the nationally known Hess Shoes.

Wholesale clothiers and dry goods firms were subsequently located here, one of whom, Alexander Falk, left his name in a tiled entrance platform, ca. 1919. Emmanuel Carton, proprietor of Baltimore Dry Goods, owned the structure in 1958, and in 1983 the property passed to Bernard Carton, owner of 407 West Baltimore Street; the two structures were joined at that time.

6. 412 WEST BALTIMORE STREET, 1857
Demolished, see preface

The building on the right in the photograph, the oldest complete cast-iron front surviving in Baltimore, was originally much more elaborate, as illustrated in city reporter John C. Gobright's 1858 *The Monumental City or Baltimore Guide Book,* which described it as "Byzantine style." The window tracery contributed to its overall busy appearance, but by 1891, when the structure was shown in "Lloyd's Baltimore Elevated Building Map," the windows had been changed to their present arrangement. Over the next century, almost all of the exterior embellishment disappeared as well, as is obvious from the 1913 photograph, which shows it still intact. This included rope molding and other decoration on the columns, Corinthian capitals, large consoles supporting cornices at all levels, applied filigree ornamentation over the arches (except at the fourth story), and antefixae above the roofline. About 1940, a new storefront was applied over the original iron one; it consisted of black Carrara glass panels, plate glass windows, and a central doorway.

The structure was originally built for Blair and Company, manufacturer of gas fittings, and the September 10, 1857, issue of the Baltimore *Sun,* noting its completion, provided some rare details of the construction and interior arrangement. The team that put up the building comprised F. H. B. Boyd, carpenter and superintendent; H. & J. Kragen, bricklayers; Sanson T. Farrand, ironworker; A. & J. Evans, plasterers; J. H. Johnson, roofer; J. W. Meyers, paperhanger; and John Hays, painter. The owners chose colors of green and bronze for the exterior.

On the inside, they installed the production facilities in the basement. The first floor was used for storage and packaging. A broad staircase with a ma-

hogany railing led to the second-floor show- and salesroom, its walls papered and ceiling hung with gas chandeliers. The third and fourth floors, lower in height, were used for meetings.

Joseph and Llewellyn Blair remained here only until 1860. From 1864 to 1913, Edward Reese, who during the period added his son to the firm, conducted a wholesale grocery business at this address. Reese's tenant, Morris Stulman, a dealer in woolen goods, acquired the property then, remaining until the 1930s and leasing space to tailoring and other garment industry-related enterprises. Morton Schenk and Company, wholesale tailor's supplies, bought the property in 1940 and still conducts business here. The iron front next door is owned by the same firm and the interior ground floors of the two buildings are joined.

Photo: Aaron Levin.

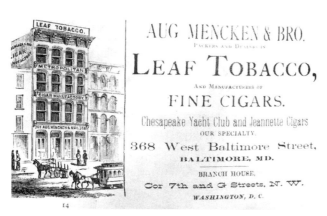

Illustration: The Peale Museum, Baltimore City Life Museums.

7. 414 WEST BALTIMORE STREET, 1876
Demolished, see Preface

At the instant I first became aware of the cosmos we all infest I was sitting in my mother's lap and blinking at a great burst of lights, some of them red and others green, but most of them only the bright yellow of flaring gas. The time: the evening of Thursday, September 13, 1883, which was the day after my third birthday. The place: a ledge outside the second-story front windows of my father's cigar factory at 368 Baltimore street, Baltimore, Maryland, U.S.A., fenced off from space and disaster by a sign bearing the majestic legend: AUG. MENCKEN & BRO. The occasion: the third and last annual Summer Nights' Carnival of the Order of Orioles, a society that adjourned sine die, with a thumping deficit, the very next morning . . .

—H. L. Mencken, *Happy Days*

1913 photo: Maryland Historical Society, Baltimore.

Mencken took his first sentient look at downtown Baltimore—and began to create a universe—from the cast-iron-front building on the left in the photograph. (When the city's streets were renumbered in 1887, 368 became 414 West Baltimore Street.)

It was known as the Joshua Robinson and Company Building for its first tenant, a manufacturer of iron stoves and household tinware whose products were sold in several southern states. The Robinson firm had been resident on the site since 1868, but remained only two years in the new building before moving on. The Mencken brothers were there in the mid-1880s, and in the '90s G. W. R. George and Company, boot and shoe jobbers, were the principal tenants. Dry goods merchants and clothing manufacturers moved in early in this century. In 1920 the Paymer Brothers, Morris and Louis, bought 414 West Baltimore Street and made pants there until the late 1950s, sharing the premises with tailors and other clothing industry firms. Morton Schenk acquired a half-interest in the building in 1937 and took over complete ownership in 1959.

The facade is almost identical to 407 West Baltimore Street on the opposite side. The building is currently used for storage.

8. McCRORY'S, 121 NORTH HOWARD STREET, CIRCA 1875

This handsome iron front was erected to house the firm of George Knipp and Brother, manufacturers of home and office furnishings and gas lighting fixtures. In 1929, the J. G. McCrory Company, nationally recognized retailers, moved to this location, connected 121 North Howard Street to a pair of adjoining structures to the south, and unified the facades with a two-story false front. This was updated in the late 1970s with brick and metal paneling, but preservationists at that time convinced the firm not to cover the upper stories of the buildings as well. The visible cast iron raises the question of how much is still left underneath.

What can be seen is impressive: geometric friezes, Corinthian columns, paneled piers with heraldic shields, and large brackets under a deep cornice. With minor exceptions, these elements also appeared on the Fava Fruit Company Building, an important structure that stood in the 200 block of South Charles Street from about 1869 to 1976, when it was dismantled and stored (see page xii). The same foundry probably cast both buildings. Current plans call for the restored Fava

facade to be reassembled in a different configuration at the Baltimore City Life Museums.

9. 235 NORTH GAY STREET, CIRCA 1875

The single bay of cast iron that wraps around the north side here to create an arcaded effect must have been even more impressive before the ground floor was filled in with brick, metal, and Carrara glass around 1940. The large window openings and the extra expanse of plate glass would have brought plenty of daylight into the storefront and loft floors of M. Rosenblatt, clothiers, tenants in the 1890s when Emanuel Schloss owned 235 North Gay Street.

Several elements of the Italianate facade—the columns, side piers with recessed panels, and heraldic shields—resemble those of the McCrory's and Fava Fruit Company buildings. A powerful cast-iron cornice with its large supporting brackets and modillions continues down the side of the building where metal hood moldings frame the windows at the second and third levels.

About 1940, 235 North Gay Street was joined, inside and out, with its neighbor at 233 North Gay, a Federal style brick row house probably dating from the 1840s. Anthony R. Spartana, founder of an electronics supply business, purchased the property in 1974. This and 353 North Gay Street, in the next block, are the only cast-iron fronts that remain in this once-thriving business district, formerly known as Oldtown, site of the earliest settlement of Baltimore.

10. 353 NORTH GAY STREET, 1871
FRANK E. DAVIS, ARCHITECT.
VARIETY IRON WORKS, FOUNDRY.

"On every hand the business streets of Old Town evince a spirit of advanced improvement. Dwellings continue to give way to stylish business improvements," said the Baltimore *Sun* on September 15, 1871. The Old Town Savings Bank, erected twenty years after the Sun Iron Building, was the first iron front east of the Jones Falls and the inspiration for several others nearby. But its two full metal facades make it unique in Baltimore.

The savings institution opened for business about 1857 and bought the lot on Gay Street roughly four years later, but the Civil War delayed construction plans. After the war, a three-story corner building was erected, fronting 30 feet on Gay Street and 100 feet on Exeter Street. The architect, Frank E. Davis (1839–1921), was born in Ellicott City, and designed numerous religious, commercial, and municipal structures in Baltimore and elsewhere in Maryland. R. G. Smyser, the founder, provided many of the city's iron fronts via his Variety Iron Works in York, Pennsylvania.

The corner banking room, with marble counters and tile floors, shared the ground floor with the drug and apothecary shop of Metzger and Stephenson, which faced Gay Street. Offices were on the second floor. The third floor was given over to a lecture and concert hall that seated 400. Druggist Franklin Metzger later occupied this space. Another tenant, until about 1940, was the Old Town Merchants and Manufacturers Association. Meanwhile, the bank moved elsewhere. The present owner of the building, a wholesale tobacco and confectionery distributor, acquired it in 1988.

The bank's original classical central portico and plate glass windows on either side have been removed and the entrance covered with brick. The same sort of treatment has been extended to the Exeter Street ground floor, but the upper levels fully express the building's cast-iron framework. Columns, capitals, and arches are reminiscent of 409 and 414 West Baltimore Street, with the addition of panels decorating the spandrels. The cornice is probably galvanized sheet metal. A single scrolled console marks the corner of the Gay Street elevation.

11. 202-206 WEST PRATT STREET, CIRCA 1870 BARTLETT, ROBBINS & CO., FOUNDRY.

The beautiful and refined ironwork of these Corinthian columns best illustrates the expressiveness of a material known primarily for its strength. They are exact replicas of the ones shown on Plate 3 of the Hayward, Bartlett & Co. catalog (page 85). More problematic are the cast-iron hood moldings over the windows on the upper floors, which may or may not have been supplied by the foundry.

The Italianate style building is nine bays wide, divided in thirds by interior party walls that are reflected outside by the wider iron columns of the storefront. Originally it housed three separate businesses. Maurice Laupenheimer & Bro., wholesale druggists, were the first listed tenants, 1879–1881, at No. 202, the easternmost address. They were succeeded in 1885 by a man who sold undertaker's supplies. In the 1920s, it was a wholesale shoe operation, and in 1940 a restaurant.

A wine and liquor firm occupied No. 204, in the middle, at the turn of the century. Later on, wholesale produce and poultry dealers were the tenants. In the late nineteenth century, another wholesale drug firm did business in No. 206; in the 1920s, bottler's supplies were sold there and, in 1940, contractor's supplies.

The ironwork was carefully preserved and the reconstructed features, such as the wooden storefront cornice, were made clearly distinguishable from the original when the entire structure was renovated and turned into a restaurant in 1981.

12. JOHNSTON BUILDING,
26-30 SOUTH HOWARD STREET, 1880
JACKSON C. GOTT, ARCHITECT.
VARIETY IRON WORKS, FOUNDRY.

Handsome, fraternal, the Johnston and Rombro buildings guard either side of Cider Alley like sentinels from a former age. They had the same developer, the Johnston Brothers, the same architect, and the same foundry. Both are double warehouses.

Contemporary news accounts actually refer to the Johnston Building, which is older by a year, as two warehouses. The repetitive nameplates at the top and the inscribed cornice return on the alley side designating it the "Johnston Buildings," plural, reinforce this idea. The dividing wall is expressed on the exterior as a central pilaster.

The style is High Victorian Eclectic; red brick and stone trim are the materials of the polychromatic, richly detailed upper facade which offers subtle variations in plane and a full range of window treatments.

Photo: Aaron Levin.

Ten column units—although one of them has been replaced with an I beam—define the neo-Grec iron storefront. The structural columns continue above the capitals, surrounded by rectangular casing with colonnettes, and extend down through the bases, one of which bears the foundry's casting mark. The spandrel beam they support also has an external jacket with a serrated lower edge.

Because the iron is deteriorated, though not irreparably, it is possible to analyze the support system. Each column is part of a structural unit, open at the rear, that is two feet deep, the depth of the fascia beam, which is also hollow and contains an I beam. The voids at the back of the column units and around the overhead I beam have been filled in with brick. Thus, the half-inch-thick decorative iron forms an envelope for the masonry and together they resist the weight of the upper four floors—a dramatic demonstration of cast iron's compressive strength.

The foundry, the Variety Iron Works of York, Pennsylvania, had an office at 4 Light Street, Baltimore, which accounted for a fourth of its sales. The company also did a substantial business supplying one of New York's large dealers in architectural ironwork. Obtaining most of their raw material from the Ashland Iron Furnace, north of Cockeysville, they specialized in architectural and ornamental items, such as columns and beams, stairways and shutters, and also turned out machinery, millwork, and entire iron buildings.

During his long career, architect Jackson C. Gott (1828–1909) designed several houses, commercial structures, industrial plants, railroad stations, college buildings, and Masonic temples throughout Maryland. He was a prominent Mason and an active Democrat, which may have accounted for his numerous public commissions. The Johnston Building is considered one of Gott's outstanding works; he is also known for the 1893 design of the Maryland Penitentiary in Baltimore. A bachelor who lived in downtown hotels most of his life, he "was a well known figure about town," according to the Baltimore *Sun.*

The earliest occupants of the Johnston Building were in the apparel business. The major tenant in the northern half was the G. S. Howser Company, dealers in hats, caps, and straw goods; and in the southern, Charles Weiller and Sons, wholesalers of "cloths, cassimeres, and vestings." By 1898, other clothing concerns had replaced them, and after the turn of the century, cigar and tobacco companies moved in. In 1904, the tenant in the southern half was Samuel Hecht, Jr., & Sons, carpet importers and jobbers. This and other Hecht family enterprises were the ancestors of the Hecht's department stores. In the 1940s and 1950s, wholesale furniture firms occupied the Johnston Building. It awaits redevelopment.

13. ROMBRO BUILDING,
22-24 SOUTH HOWARD STREET, 1881
JACKSON C. GOTT, ARCHITECT.
VARIETY IRON WORKS, FOUNDRY.

A year younger, a story taller, and more colorfully arrayed than its neighbor across the alley, the Rombro Building was higher still when it was built. The 1891 "Lloyd's Baltimore Elevated Building Map" for this block depicts what seems to be a pair of Greek temples perched atop the structure. At some point, they were removed.

The architect clearly went all out for his later creation. Again, a central pilaster divides the facade. Sixteen sets of brick piers, pilasters, and caps grip the stone columns, with their heavy bases and capitals, to form column units analogous to the iron ones in the storefront below. Just one of the latter, with a portion of the spandrel beam, is seen at the north door. Four brooding, stylized, sheet-metal gables regard this variegated assemblage from above.

The iron storefront is similar to the Johnston Building's, except that it has been mostly covered with cosmetic materials. The north entrance leads to a small

vestibule containing an elevator and stairway; a similar entrance was located at the building's south side. The floors above are mostly open loft space. Instead of a dividing wall, seven iron columns run down the center of each one except the sixth, which has wooden posts.

The building cost the Johnston Brothers, developers, $50,000. Henry Elliott Johnston and Josiah Lee Johnston, his younger brother, had inherited their father's investment banking business and renamed it Johnston Brothers and Company. In the late 1870s, they assembled roughly half-a-dozen lots on either side of Cider Alley and in 1880–1881 built the Johnston and Rombro buildings. Harriet Lane, Henry's wife, was an equal partner in the properties.

She was the orphaned niece of James Buchanan, a bachelor, who raised and educated her, and on becoming president in 1857, brought her into the White House as official hostess. Pretty and vivacious, she married Henry Elliott Johnston in 1866. When their

two sons died of rheumatic fever as teenagers, the bereaved parents established the Harriet Lane Home in 1883, and after their deaths, the Johnston and Rombro buildings with the rest of the estate became its property. Trustees sold the two warehouse buildings in 1919; the roughly $125,000 in proceeds formed part of the endowment. The Harriet Lane Home in the meantime had affiliated with the Johns Hopkins Hospital, and subsequently made major contributions to the development of pediatrics in America.

The most important tenant—and virtually the only one until Morris Rombro bought the building in 1919—was Carroll, Adams & Co., manufacturers and wholesalers of boots and shoes, who kept a dozen traveling salesmen on the road in the Midwest and South. Clark, Perry and Company, in the same business, also occupied the building initially. The firm of Rombro Brothers, shirtmakers, composed of Morris and his brother Jacob, posted their name at the top of the edifice and remained here until 1958, about as many years as their predecessors. In 1963, the David & Annie Abrams Realty Corp., owners of the Abell Building, acquired the structure. Current plans call for its rehabilitation.

14. ABELL BUILDING,
329-335 WEST BALTIMORE STREET,
CIRCA 1878
GEORGE A. FREDERICK, ARCHITECT.
BARTLETT, ROBBINS & CO., FOUNDRY.

Exuberant architecture and outstanding ironwork are the hallmarks of the Abell Building, the finest surviving Victorian warehouse in Baltimore. Its corner location and size—six stories high and a full block deep—add to its impact.

George A. Frederick was the architect of Baltimore's City Hall, completed in 1875, and was named a fellow of the American Institute of Architects in 1877. He designed this building as an investment property for A. S. Abell, proprietor of the Baltimore *Sun*. The cast-iron storefront's neo-Grec precision and sheer 276-foot extent, covering three sides of the building, make it unique in the city despite the intervention of modern metal paneling that partially or totally obscures the ground floors on Baltimore and Eutaw streets.

However, the one-and-a-half stories of cast iron (due to the slope of the site) facing Redwood Street are fully exposed and illustrate the elements of neo-Grec design: flattened segmental arches, incised ornament, and stylized classical and geometric details. Bartlett,

Robbins & Co. contemporaneously produced the ironwork for the Peabody Library in the neo-Grec style. They also furnished some of the ironwork for the City Hall dome, as did its designer, Wendel Bollman, an engineer and bridge-builder.

But the inspiration for neo-Grec was more structural than stylistic. As defined by Labrouste, Viollet-le-Duc, and other French architects working in the mid-nineteenth century, it stood for a return to the pure architectural logic of the Greeks. (This could be most directly achieved with metal, as demonstrated by Labrouste in the thin cast-iron columns and vaults for the reading room of the Bibliotheque Nationale in Paris, 1862–1868; and by Viollet-le-Duc, who in his writings compared the structural systems of a Gothic cathedral with those of an iron-framed building.)

Above the ironwork, the architect combined a variety of materials to create a dazzling polychrome effect in the High Victorian Italianate style: enlivening the decorative Baltimore red brick are white marble, bluestone, and terra cotta trim. The pediment in the center of the Eutaw Street elevation once held the legend "Abell Building." The low, set-back sixth story was added sometime later.

The Abell Building is a double warehouse with the bearing wall expressed externally by prominent central piers on the Baltimore Street and Redwood Street facades. The interior, according to an early account, had hardwood floors and woodwork, hydraulic elevators, fire- and burglarproof vaults, and 13,000 square feet of basement under the warehouse and adjoining sidewalks.

Since its opening, the Abell Building has housed an endless parade of tenants, most but not all associated with the garment industry. The needle trades were well represented at the beginning; however, early neighbors included a cigar business, a carpenter and builder, a roofing concern, a saddle and harness maker, and a confectionery. The Isaac Friedenwald Company, the largest and best-equipped printers, lithographers, and engravers in the South, according to *Frank Leslie's Illustrated Newspaper*, moved in in 1898. A long association with the insurance industry started the same year; agents and brokers for various firms occupied offices through the early decades of the twentieth century.

In 1914, the Abell Building was sold to Jacob Epstein. He located his American Wholesale Corporation here, which made clothing for his retail outlet, the Baltimore Bargain House. The current owners, the David & Annie Abrams Realty Corp., acquired the building in 1957. It is still occupied by clothing manufacturers and related firms.

15. 318 WEST REDWOOD STREET, 1852
DIXON, BALBIRNIE, AND DIXON,
ARCHITECTS.
BENJAMIN S. BENSON, FOUNDRY.

Hidden away on Redwood Street, making up the ground-floor rear of a drab, five-story building whose principal elevation is at 321 West Baltimore Street, stands the city's oldest cast-iron storefront. Yet when it opened in March 1852, according to press accounts, this address formed part of the "finest block of commercial buildings" in Baltimore. To the west were two more structures, also extending through to Balti-

more Street. All three buildings, built as a complex, had cast-iron storefronts front and back. They were products of the foundry of Benjamin S. Benson, who had just completed the exterior ironwork on the Sun Iron Building. The adjacent buildings have been demolished and all that remains of the original ironwork is a pair of columns and two recessed-panel piers with massive scrolled consoles at 318 West Redwood Street.

This part of the complex was built by Chauncey Brooks, prominent local merchant and president of the Western Bank and the Baltimore and Ohio Railroad in the 1850s. It housed a series of enterprises in the garment trade operated by Brooks and his associates during that and the following decade, mostly boots and shoes, hats, and dry goods. The only tenants of record at the Redwood Street address (in 1879) were a candy maker and, on the second floor, a factory that produced gilt and walnut molding. The storefront is now vacant; its last occupant was the Good Humor Cafe.

16. 419 WEST BALTIMORE STREET,
CIRCA 1875
BARTLETT, ROBBINS & CO., FOUNDRY (?)

As Baltimore expanded westward, its residential areas were overtaken by commercialization. The building at 419 West Baltimore Street was originally a typical Federal style home, erected during the first quarter of the nineteenth century. It probably had two dormers above the roofline and an off-center entrance aligned with one of the upper sets of windows. Many such houses, occupied by middle-class merchants and their families, once lined the streets of the city.

During the 1870s, however, this one was drastically altered by the insertion of a cast-iron storefront and the conversion of the upper floors to commercial use. The iron columns and pilasters, with simple raised molded panels and central bull's-eye motif, but missing their capital leaves, so closely resemble a stock item in the Hayward, Bartlett catalog (Plate No. 2, page 84) that the foundry was almost surely the source.

The building's upper stories are of brick laid in Flemish bond. Because the converted row house lacked the open floor space and oversize windows of the neighboring loft buildings occupied by the major clothing manufacturers, it attracted tenants with smaller operations.

The first long-term occupant after the conversion was Joshua Robinson and Company, iron stove and tinware manufacturer. This was the firm's third documented move on West Baltimore Street. In 1866 they were in a three-story brick dwelling at 307-309 before it was replaced with the present iron front. The business was located at 414 West Baltimore from 1868 to 1878, during which time the structure at that address was evidently removed and the existing iron front erected. Their 1882 takeover of 419 West Baltimore, where they remained for almost ten years, represented a shift to smaller quarters.

Another stove and furnace dealer, Frank J. Murphy, occupied 419 West Baltimore Street after that, and extended his operations to 415 and 417. On "Lloyd's Baltimore Elevated Building Map" (page 62), 419 West Baltimore Street is the structure farthest to the left below the label "South Paca Street."

Small enterprises, gathering at the periphery of Baltimore's large garment industry, which was centered to the east and south, followed in the twentieth century: tailor's trimmings, notions, button companies, etc. The present tenant carries on the tradition.

17. 423 WEST BALTIMORE STREET, CIRCA 1876; RENOVATED 1893 LOUIS J. GINTER, RENOVATION ARCHITECT.
Demolished, see Preface

Architect Ginter and builder Thomas L. Jones spent $9,000 in 1893 drastically altering a three-story brick warehouse on this site. The result was unusual, to say the least.

The original building housed Gable and Beacham's sash and door factory from 1879 to 1881. Then the Southern Bottling Company moved in, sold 4,000 barrels of their trademark Rochester brand beer the first year of operation, and as quickly disappeared. Liquor dealers succeeded them. In 1888, the warehouse changed ownership, and five years after that, received a new look. "The building has an open iron front with a dome, which gives it a very showy appearance," observed the Baltimore *Sun*.

The cast-iron storefront was added at that time, judging by its style. It was probably rearranged in recent years: the additional column to the left of the secondary entrance is actually wood, but so cleverly mimics the others that it is impossible to tell the difference without a magnet.

The greatest alterations in 1893 were higher up. Two floors were added to the original three, but rather than receding in height as they ascended, they were made 25 percent higher with transomed windows. The entire facade must have been removed during this process, as evidenced by the vast difference in its fenestration compared to the structures on either side. The walls were raised and the entire space between them filled with a wood-framed window grid, covered with sheet metal. It reflects the influence of Chicago's Commercial style buildings.

But the look, with its grotesque decoration, is purely Baltimorean. The storefront's cast-iron consoles are echoed at the third level and again below the

kitchen cabinets, stoves, electric ventilators, builder's supplies, and musical instruments joined them in the following decade, and the diverse mix of tenants continued into the 1960s. Now the loft floors appear vacant; a street-level restaurant remains.

18. 414-418 WEST LOMBARD STREET, 1890
CHARLES L. CARSON, ARCHITECT.

Fresh winds were blowing in American architecture when this building went up, mostly from Chicago where H. H. Richardson's massive Marshall Field Wholesale Store had been completed three years earlier. That was the model for Baltimore's first Commercial style warehouse. Carson chose to do his version in brick, with sandstone trim, terra cotta details, and heavy cast-iron framing for the ground-floor entrance and plate glass windows.

By this time, the metal was no longer integral to the building's exterior support system, and its only function here is to act as a decorated framework for the windows and doorways. The columns are embossed with ornamentation; rows of stylized rivets and rosettes enliven the spandrel beams. Above the powerful, rhythmic arches of the upper facade, and the characteristic row of smaller windows at the top, a sheet metal cornice wraps around the corner of the building, extending across a 1914 addition, the Marlboro Building at 410-412 West Lombard Street.

Carson, the son of David Carson, builder of Waverly Terrace (see page 56), was the city's leading practitioner of the Romanesque Revival and a nation-

roofline where they appear in the enlarged form typical of the Neoclassical Revival. The facade is crowned by an interrupted cornice and exaggerated finials, all in sheet metal.

The changes were doubtless designed to accommodate the garment industry. The first tenants after the renovation were clothing manufacturers who remained until 1907. Between 1908 and 1912, Polan, Katz and Company, prominent umbrella manufacturers, had their facilities here. Twenty years later, in another location, they were making three million umbrellas annually and leading the country in production; the name of their product line was the Reigning Beauty. (Baltimore claimed to have produced America's first umbrella in 1797.)

In the 1920s, a succession of tailors, woolens brokers, and pants and shirt manufacturers plied their trades on the well-lit upper floors. Firms dealing in

ally known architect. He died the year after this building was finished; the addition was designed by his former partner, Joseph Evans Sperry. (There were iron columns on the first floor of 414-418 West Lombard, but the upper loft floors were supported by wooden posts and beams; Sperry's addition had structural steel throughout the interior.)

The original building was built for the Strouse Brothers, makers of men's suits and overcoats, and they did business here until 1920, when the firm was liquidated. The building at 410-412 West Lombard Street was constructed for the Marlboro Shirt Company, which occupied both buildings from 1920 up into the 1970s and became one of the nation's largest shirt manufacturers. In the following decade the entire premises, renamed Marlboro Square, was renovated as an apartment building at a cost of $7.25 million; a postmodern open light court was created in the center. Burns and Geiger and the Columbia Design Collective were the renovation architects.

19. 40-42 SOUTH PACA STREET, 1887

A Victorian double warehouse a la mode, but more restrained than some of its predecessors, the Strauss Building, as it was once known, presents five floors of fine brickwork with stone and terra cotta details over a ground floor that displays a pair of functional iron storefronts. A sheet metal cornice defines the roofline.

The initial tenants were the Kinney Tobacco Company, cigarette manufacturers, and M. S. Levy and

Sons, makers of straw hats. The Strauss Brothers, clothing manufacturers, moved in later.

A century ago, Paca Street between Baltimore and Pratt streets was the heart of the clothing manufacturing district in Baltimore, a multimillion-dollar-a-year industry employing thousands of workers. In the open loft floors of these buildings, women sat at row upon row of clattering sewing machines. But as the owners, mostly Russian Jews, retired, the companies died or relocated, and the machines fell silent.

After many years of garment industry use, 40-42 South Paca Street, and the two contiguous buildings to the north, were acquired about 1977 by Inner Harbor Loft Associates for conversion into apartments. The exteriors of the buildings were cleaned, the bricks repointed, and the interiors completely renovated. The new spaces, featuring twelve- to fourteen-foot ceilings, mezzanine levels, and exposed brick walls, were quickly rented, and the buildings—Baltimore's first loft-to-residences conversion—became one of the city's most successful adaptive reuse projects.

20. 509-511 WEST LOMBARD STREET, 1893
VARIETY IRON WORKS, FOUNDRY (?)

A typical Baltimore double warehouse with an iron storefront is here expressed in the Commercial style. The fluted columns on the ground floor, echoed by cast-iron colonnettes on the fourth, have tall bases, decorative bands midway up the shaft, and scrolled capitals.

The building was erected by Elias Rosenbaum as a speculative venture, and functioned until recently as a factory with street-level showrooms. The first tenants were the Burroughs Brothers, manufacturers of "medicinal extracts," who soon purchased the structure and occupied it until 1917. At that time, August Maag, a manufacturer of utensils for bakers, confectioners, and ice cream makers, rented the building, remaining until 1930. Next, the Turner-White Casket Company bought it and stayed until its sale to the University of Maryland in 1968. Since that time, the building has housed the university's bookstore and development offices.

The interior was altered after a 1969 fire; however, the cast-iron columns supporting the wooden beams on all floors (except the sixth, which has wooden posts) are still in place. These columns, some of which are eight feet high, are embossed with the letters "EGS Sons." This stood for Edward G. Smyser & Sons' Variety Iron Works of York, Pennsylvania, which had a Baltimore sales office. It is possible that they produced all of the ironwork for this building.

21. 519-525 WEST PRATT STREET, CIRCA 1892

The adjoining structures on the southeast corner of Pratt and Greene streets, now known as the Greenehouse Loft Apartments, once housed the factory and warehouse operations of the Erlanger enterprises,

makers of the famed B.V.D. brand underwear. The easternmost, a six-story Commercial style brick warehouse, is the older and handsomer.

At street level, a triple complement of beautiful ringed columns and decorated spandrel beams compose a tripartite cast-iron storefront. The proliferation of sidewalk vault lights—small circular pieces of glass set into the pavement to admit light to the lower level—is a sure sign that the basement was also used in the manufacturing process. The interior support system consisted of iron columns on the first floor and

ceased in 1951 when the corporation was sold. Small industrial firms then occupied the buildings until they were acquired in 1979 by Inner Harbor Loft Associates for rehabilitation and conversion to apartments.

22. 118-120 NORTH PACA STREET, 1883

Down the street from the venerable Lexington Market, Ormond Hammond bought a piece of property, put up a building, and opened a slaughterhouse. In 1884 his firm, Hammond and Wilmer, was listed as being in the wholesale meat business at this address. Three years later, reorganized as the National Consumers Meat Company, they operated ten retail stores throughout the city. The Charles Rohr Packing Company bought the business about 1890, and ran it for a similar length of time, but shortly before the turn of the century, the building was converted to laundry use.

wooden ones on the open loft floors above; the floors themselves were maple.

In the late nineteenth century, Charles Erlanger, brother Abraham, and brother-in-law Herman Bonheim founded Erlanger, Bonheim and Company, wholesale jobbers. Later, as Erlanger Brothers, they made overalls and work shirts. Later still, having acquired the firm of Bradley, Vorhees, and Day, they began producing B.V.D. underwear. There is some dispute about the origin of the initials, but no question that the product—knee-length drawers that did away with the old-fashioned union suits—revolutionized the American underwear business and gained a worldwide reputation. (The creators themselves were modest about their contribution; Charles Erlanger once silenced his son, who was holding forth on the importance of the B.V.D. company, by saying "Let's stop that line. All we ever really did was to cut drawers shorter.")

The corporate offices were in New York, but B.V.D.s were made on West Pratt Street for fifty years. The business expanded into the adjacent buildings, and the B.V.D. Corporation, as it was known after 1929, produced pajamas, robes, and sportswear, and helped to introduce men's topless swim trunks and women's one-piece bathing suits. Local operations

The Star Laundry Company was the first new tenant, replaced after 1902 by the Sanitary Laundry Company, which left painted signs on the outside walls. By 1911, a gas mantle manufacturer had set up shop on the third floor and it was there, or in the fifth-floor laundry workroom, that a fire started in February 1914. Between thirty and seventy-five young women were at work in the laundry at the time; they all fled the building except one, Lizzie Manford, who had to be removed by firemen. The tenants abandoned the structure after that and it remained vacant until 1928 when a paper box company moved in and stayed until the 1970s. Now it is empty again.

A substantial commercial building, it reflects the influence of the Queen Anne style, popular in the late nineteenth century. The upper facade offers some fine brickwork with terra cotta and brownstone trim, and the cast-iron storefront features a complex molded metal cornice. A renovation program is being discussed.

23. 100-102 NORTH GREENE STREET, 1895

In its heyday, the Swiss Steam Laundry Building played an important part in the clothing industry, then the city's largest. Manufacturers sent new shirts here

to be washed before distributing them to wholesale and retail outlets. Each floor had its purpose: washing took place in the basement, sorting on the first floor, dyeing on the second, ironing on the third, drying on the fourth, packing on the fifth, and more sorting on the sixth. In 1898, the laundry was one of the country's largest, with 200 employees and a capacity of 7,200 shirts a day.

Furniture manufacturer Charles T. Bagby erected the building as a speculative venture and leased it in 1896 to the Swiss Steam Laundry Company. By 1900, the Elite Laundry was conducting the cleaning and dyeing business, and the Swiss Manufacturing Company sold laundry supplies. The Elite Laundry expanded and merged with similar operations in the early 1900s. They left the building in 1915; clothing manufacturers and other firms moved in. Recently, new owners acquired the structure and converted it to other uses.

It is a typical Baltimore double warehouse with a pronounced central pier and a strong set of arches at the fifth-floor level. The materials are bright red brick with stone trim in the Commercial style. The floors decrease in height as they ascend and are capped by a deep cornice of sheet metal. A handsome and ornate cast-iron storefront faces Greene Street, and there are iron columns throughout the interior.

24. ENGINE HOUSE NO. 8, 1031 WEST MULBERRY STREET, 1871
Demolished, see Preface

In response to expanding residential development on Baltimore's west side in the late 1860s, the mayor and city council organized Engine Company No. 8. This was its home until 1912 when the company relocated. It lingers still, the sole surviving example in the city of a public building with a cast-iron front.

Even in reduced circumstances, with one of its iron columns missing, the small Italianate style firehouse rewards a second glance: the upper story has fine brickwork below a row of wooden consoles supporting a sheet metal cornice and parapet. At street-level, the cast-iron front clearly reflects the building's use—its central bay, topped by a keystone and bull's eye panel bearing the legend "No. 8," is slightly more than twice the width of those on either side in order to accommodate the fire equipment.

The columns and arches appear to have been derived from three illustrations in the Bartlett, Robbins & Co. catalog (Plates 4, 6, and 12, pages 85, 87), a good example of how owners could create their own compositions, have the foundry execute them in metal, and then hire workmen to assemble them on-site. It might also explain why so few cast-iron buildings have listed architects. The bull's-eyes in the corner pilasters of the firehouse incorporate the figure 8.

After the engine company left, the building seems to have remained vacant until 1928, when Louis M. Helm opened a motorcycle repair shop. The upper floor functioned as headquarters for youth clubs, the Boys' Brigade, and later on, the Camp Mil-Bur Cadets. Lou's Motor Service occupied it from 1940 into the 1960s, and the building is still used for automobile repairs. A hose-drying tower that once stood on the site has been removed.

25. PORT MISSION,
813 SOUTH BROADWAY, CIRCA 1860

A century ago when Fells Point, which dates from the early eighteenth century, was an immigrant center and a hard-working waterfront, foreign sailors mingled here with neighborhood residents who were almost as new to America as they. The red and green ship's running lights on the brick facades over the

unified, but quite different, Victorian cast-iron store-fronts are a reminder that the Baltimore harbor is just a few steps away.

The first known occupant of the four-story structure, in the late 1860s, was Strauss and Bro., wholesale and retail grocers. From 1871 to 1885, it was a steam bakery. During this period, two ship's chandlers operated in the adjacent two-story building (formerly 815 South Broadway). The second of these was Giovanni Schiaffino, an Italian immigrant who brought his new bride with him to Baltimore. (This enterprising businessman served as the Italian and Spanish consul in Baltimore in the early 1900s, and as the Belgian consul during World War I.)

The Port Mission was founded in 1881, through the preachings of Chicago evangelist Dwight L. Moody, to bring the gospel to Fells Point's seamen, a rowdy group that, willingly or not, was often preyed upon by the area's bartenders, boardinghouse crimps, and prostitutes. In 1884, the Port Mission acquired the two-story building, and in 1895 connected it to the four-story warehouse next door, which they bought in 1897. (Their Women's Auxiliary in 1892 established the Anchorage nearby as a seamen's home.) The Port Mission currently offers special programs for children and ministers to those in need throughout the city.

26. 1638-1640 THAMES STREET, CIRCA 1862

In October 1862, Henry G. Tyark Deetjen bought this property on which stood "two old two story frame dwellings," according to the Baltimore *Sun*. He replaced them with the present brick edifice, incorporating an expansive cast-iron storefront to accommodate his ship's chandlery and grocery store. The structure appears on the 1869 Sachse "Bird's-Eye View of Baltimore." Deetjen left in 1871, and from 1879 to 1920 the building housed a wine and liquor business. In the latter year it was deeded to the Anchorage next door.

Established in 1892 by the Women's Auxiliary of the Port Mission, at 813 South Broadway, the purpose of the Anchorage was to "maintain under Christian influence a boarding house for seamen, a home-away-from-home, a social and recreational center where the seafarer might find safe refuge while in port." Taken over by the YMCA about 1930, the 150-bed Anchorage housed as many as 50,000 sailors a year. Rooms cost thirty-five cents a night or two dollars a week and were so small the residents nicknamed the hotel "the doghouse." They were sometimes entertained by Peabody

Institute pianists, and at Christmastime sang carols in three languages.

The hotel lasted until the mid-1950s, when the complex was turned into a cider and vinegar bottling works. In 1985, after a $3-million renovation, it reopened as a 37-room inn with prices starting at ninety dollars a night. The storefront was also returned to its original retail function. The fluted Corinthian columns and pilasters, resting on granite sills, have been restored, their missing elements recast, and the whole attractively painted.

Part Three

IRONWORK CATALOGS

These two small volumes compose the catalog of the Hayward, Bartlett (later the Bartlett, Robbins) foundry, Baltimore's premier architectural ironworks. They are rare items; no other copies are known to exist. Found in the company archives and deposited in the Peabody Library, they are reprinted here for the first time since their initial publication. That was probably in the 1850s for Volume One, and in the following decade for Volume Two. (Hayward, Bartlett & Co. became Bartlett, Robbins & Co. in 1866.)

Unlike Daniel D. Badger's famous *Illustrations of Iron Architecture*, which was published (and twice recently reissued) in large format in 1865 as a sourcebook for architects and their clients as well as an advertising medium for Badger's New York foundry, the Baltimore books were pocket catalogs, roughly three by five inches, a handy size for salesmen to carry and show to customers.

They are illustrated with the lithographs of E. Sachse and Company, creators of the well-known "Bird's-Eye View of Baltimore." Volume One depicts several examples of architectural elements: columns, arches, and entablatures, along with window lintels and hood moldings. "All were offered to the architect and his client that they might present to the public a grand facade, or what was commonly known as a 'cast-iron front,' to advertise the wealth and stability of the business behind it," said a company historian. The customer could pick and choose among these components and styles, combining a column shown in one plate with a bracket or console from another. This volume has helped architectural historians identify some of the existing Baltimore iron fronts.

The cover of Volume Two features one of the well-known pair of cast-iron Newfoundland dogs, "Sailor" and "Canton," several versions of which guarded the entrances to the various office and foundry sites in Baltimore. Symbolic of the principals' enthusiasm for duck hunting on the Chesapeake Bay, they became company talismans and "a delusion and a snare to all the dogs that pass by." (Statues of "Sailor" and "Canton" can still be seen at the Baltimore Gas and Electric Company's Spring Gardens plant. See page 21.)

This second volume presents a wide selection of the foundry's products, from cuspidors to revolving aquariums, and includes the dimensions and costs for such items as cast-iron fountains and lawn furniture, handwritten in red ink. The prices will certainly amaze the buyers of today's reproductions.

The author of the section on "Architectural Iron Work," in Horace Greeley's 1872 *The Great Industries of the United States*, was only slightly exaggerating when he concluded his tour of the foundry at Pratt and Scott streets, and his sketch of the firm, with the following observation:

> *Now, returning to the counting-room, if we sit down and consult the series of lithographs, wood cuts, and photographs laid before us, and ask any additional questions, we find that the firm can make for us a house, all complete, with walls, floors, doors, windows, roof, verandas, and balconies, cornices, and external ornaments of many kinds, vaults, and vault lights, ventilators, with fences and gates, ornamental fountains, summer house, vases, statuary, and garden seats, chairs or settees, gas and water fixtures, a heating apparatus,*

The Hayward, Bartlett and Bartlett, Robbins catalogs are reprinted with the permission of the George Peabody Library of the Johns Hopkins University.

and either kitchener, range, or cooking stove, as required, parlor stoves, or grates of any kind, ornamental brackets for shelving, hitching posts and stable fixtures, such as mangers, rack, partitions, etc., drain pipe, iron pavements, bath tubs, and plumbers' castings, and pipe of all kinds. Cast iron pots and kettles, and culinary implements of all kinds, go with the stove. Bedsteads of cast iron or wrought iron, or both, can also be furnished. In fact, in case of strict necessity, the firm of Bartlett, Robbins & Co. could turn out a dwelling which, with the addition of the necessary textile fabrics, would be surprisingly near to complete readiness for its inmates.

The catalog appears here exactly as it exists, except that four of its pages have been printed on one page of this volume. The two small books are perfect reflections of the company's straightforward approach to business and of Baltimore's unpretentious manner. As a Bartlett, Robbins spokesman replied to an inquirer about their heating plants: "We do not run this as a hobby, and do not desire to overrate the apparatus, having always preferred inviting investigation of fixtures, tested by long use, in preference to publishing."

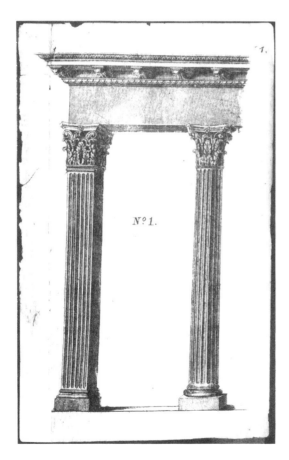

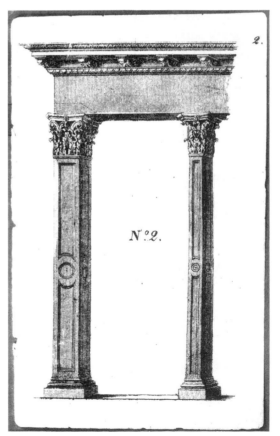

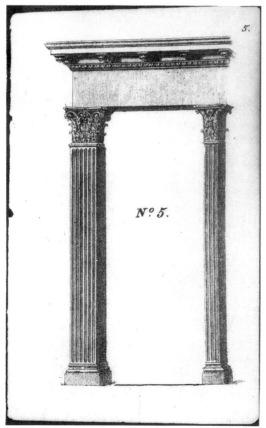

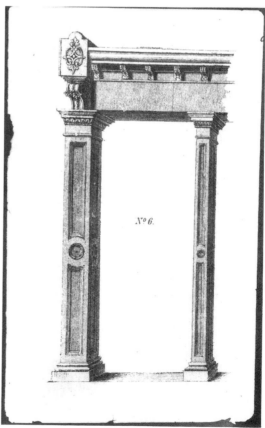

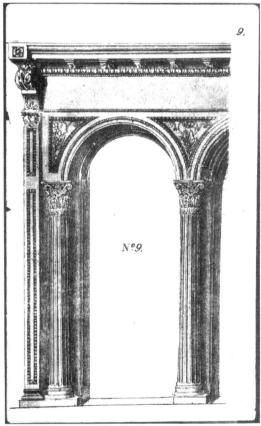

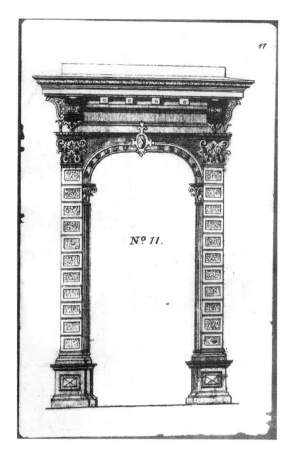

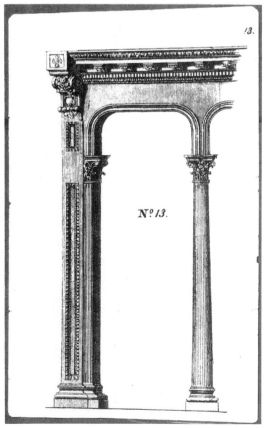

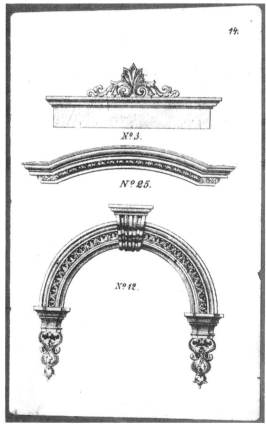

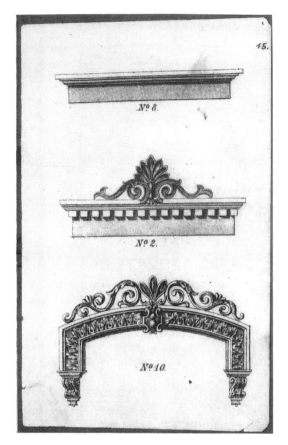

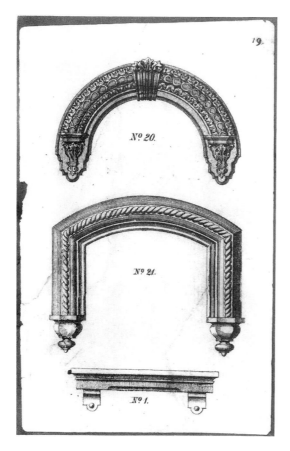

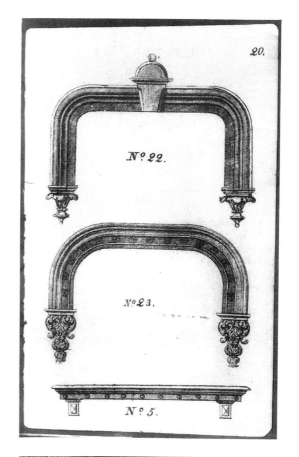

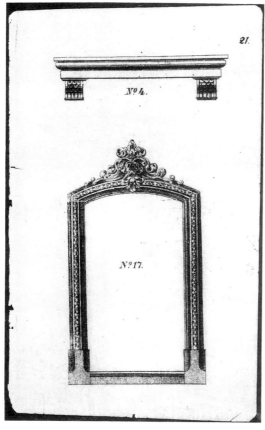

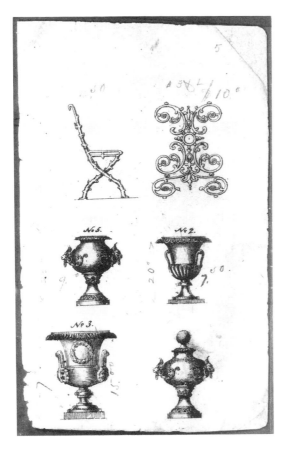

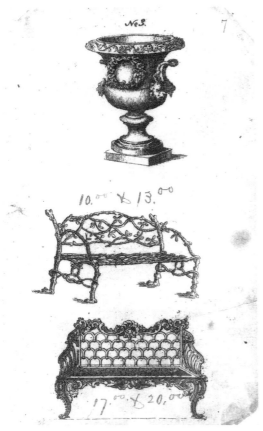

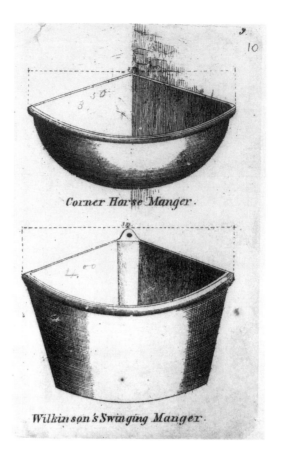

Corner Horse Manger.

Wilkinson's Swinging Manger.

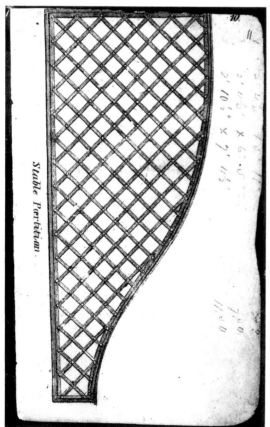

Stable Partition.

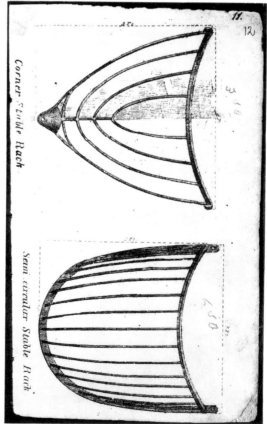

Corner Stable Rack.

Semi circular Stable Rack.

Revolving Aquarium with Pedestal.

Aquarium.

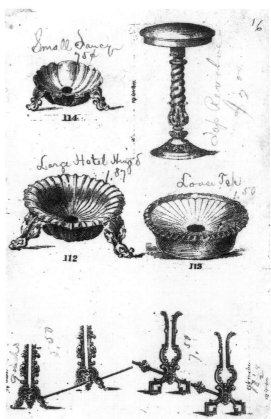

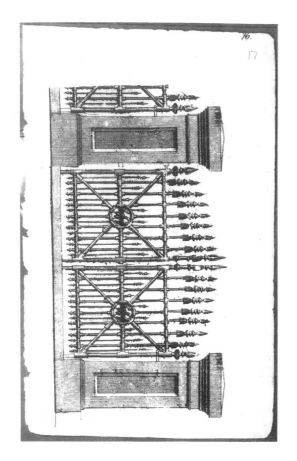

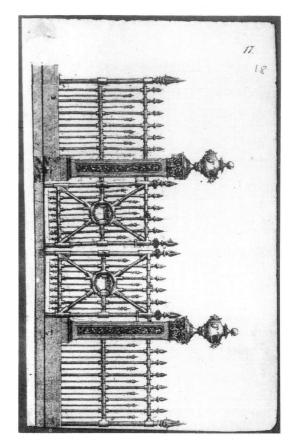

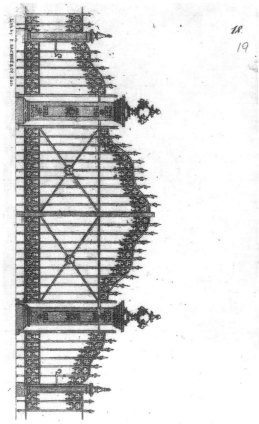

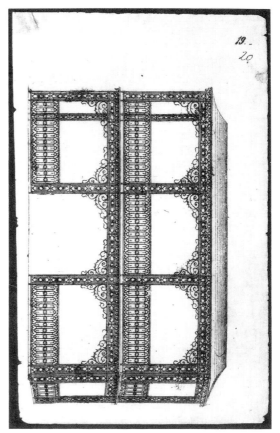

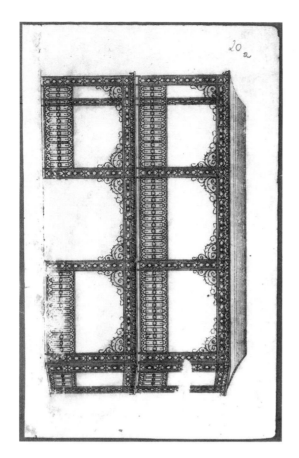

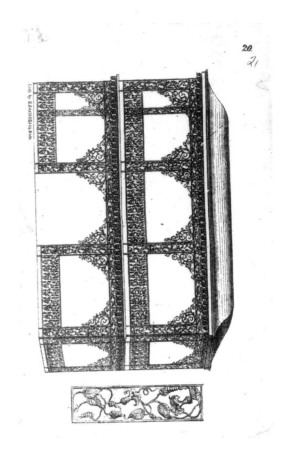

CRESTINGS FOR MANSARD OR FRENCH ROOFS.

CRESTINGS FOR MANSARD OR FRENCH ROOFS.

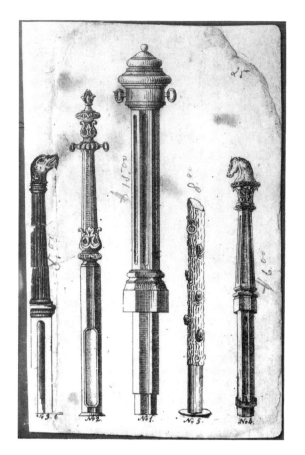

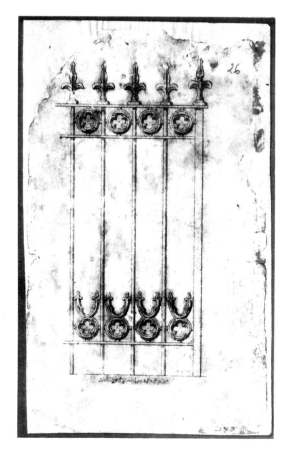

BIBLIOGRAPHY

Arthur, Eric, and Thomas Ritchie, *Iron*, Toronto: University of Toronto Press, 1982.

Badger, Daniel D., *Badger's Illustrated Catalogue of Cast-Iron Architecture*, New York: Dover, 1981.

Fairbairn, William, *On the Application of Cast and Wrought Iron to Building Purposes*, London: 1854.

Gardner, J. Starkie, *Iron Work*, London: 1892.

Gay, John, *Cast Iron*, London: John Murray, Ltd., 1985.

Gayle, Margot, and Edmund V. Gillon, Jr., *Cast-Iron Architecture in New York*, New York: Dover, 1974.

Geerlings, Gerald K., *Wrought Iron in Architecture*, New York: Scribners, 1929.

Giedion, Sigfried, *Space, Time and Architecture*, Cambridge, Mass.: Harvard University Press, 1941.

Gloag, John, and Derek Bridgwater, *A History of Cast Iron in Architecture*, London: 1948.

Hitchcock, Henry-Russell, *Architecture: Nineteenth and Twentieth Centuries*, Middlesex, England: Penguin Books, Ltd., 1958.

Kohlmaier, Georg, and Barna Von Sartory, *Houses of Glass*, Cambridge, Mass.: MIT Press, 1986.

Robertson, E. Graeme, and Joan Robertson, *Cast Iron Decoration*, New York: Whitney Library of Design, 1977.

Southwork, Susan, and Michael Southwork, *Ornamental Ironwork*, Boston: David R. Godine, 1978.

Sturges, W. Knight, *The Origins of Cast Iron Architecture in America*, New York: Da Capo Press, 1970.

Swank, James M., *History of the Manufacture of Iron in All Ages*, Philadelphia: 1884.

INDEX

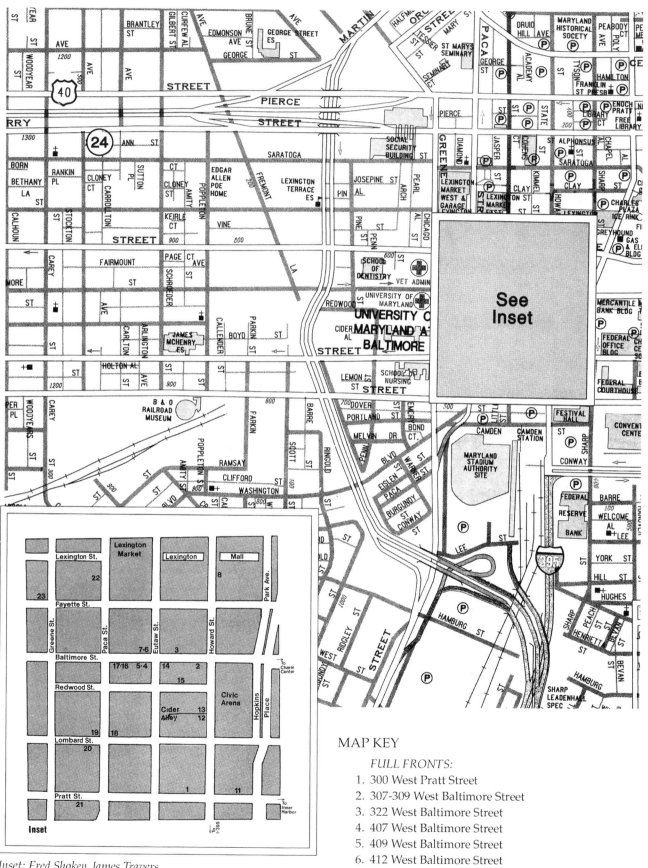

Inset: Fred Shoken, James Travers

MAP KEY

FULL FRONTS:

1. 300 West Pratt Street
2. 307-309 West Baltimore Street
3. 322 West Baltimore Street
4. 407 West Baltimore Street
5. 409 West Baltimore Street
6. 412 West Baltimore Street
7. 414 West Baltimore Street
8. McCrory's, 121 North Howard Street

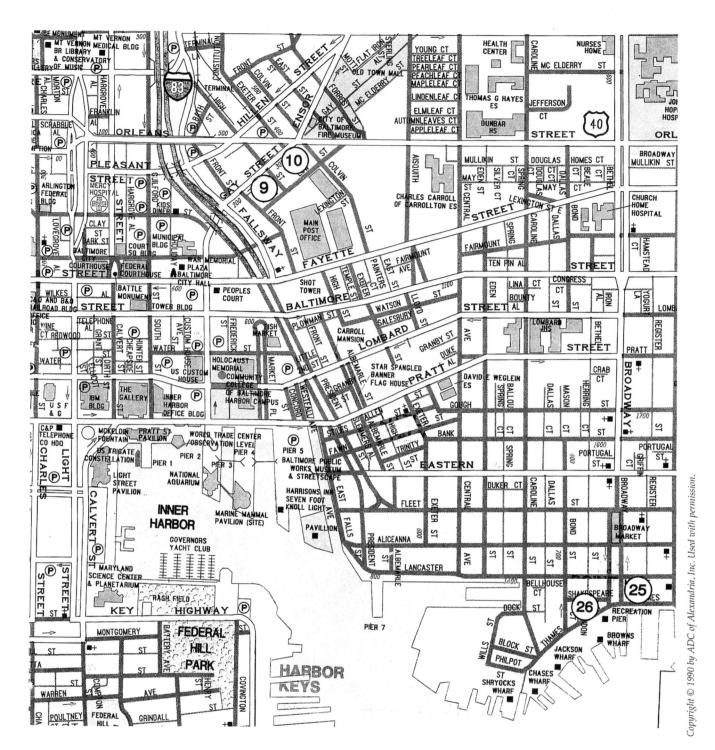

9. 235 North Gay Street

10. 353 North Gay Street

STOREFRONTS:

11. 202-206 West Pratt Street

12. Johnston Building, 26-30 South Howard Street

13. Rombro Building, 22-24 South Howard Street

14. Abell Building, 329-335 West Baltimore Street

15. 318 West Redwood Street

16. 419 West Baltimore Street

17. 423 West Baltimore Street

18. 414-418 West Lombard Street

19. 40-42 South Paca Street

20. 509-511 West Lombard Street

21. 519-525 West Pratt Street

22. 118-120 North Paca Street

23. 100-102 North Greene Street

24. Engine House No. 8, 1025-1031 West Mulberry Street

25. Port Mission, 813 South Broadway

26. 1638-1640 Thames Street